SAX
STORIES

TALES FROM AN EAST SUFFOLK TOWN

Not only are the people shy, but the spirit of the county itself is independent, capricious and elusive – if you don't treat it properly it will, like an unresponsive tortoise, retire to the seclusion of its own shell and escape you for ever. That slight animosity of Suffolk attracts the right people and repels the wrong ones.

Julian Tennyson, Suffolk Scene 1939

For my Grandmother,
Betty Moore, née Emsden,
a Saxmundham girl.

Contents

Introduction

I feel hugely privileged to have been able to write this book. Saxmundham people are often reticent when it comes to speaking about their lives. Although tall tales and gossip are as popular as they always have been, genuine life stories are rarely heard.

For people from other places, it can be frustrating. You can know someone for many years and have little clue about their lives before you met them.

Many of the characters in the book form part of a generation born around the time of the Second World War. These people grew up with rationing, before widespread TV or vehicle ownership.

Often, they began exhaustingly hard full-time work on the land or in service when they were just 14 or 15. There was no professional help for family trauma, poverty or bereavement. Support came from family and the local community. Ties were tight.

When times were tough, Saxmundham people kept their heads down and got on with it.

In East Suffolk, it's not done to boast or to brag, least of all to try and pass yourself off as something you're not. It's where the local sense of humour comes from; so dry it can pass by unnoticed unless you're properly attuned to being teased out of your pretentions.

In the mid 20th century, Saxmundham was a thriving market town, packed with people and industry. Less than half the population of today, yet important enough to host the Suffolk Show.

I haven't written this book as a mournful longing for times gone by. I'd love to have seen the Suffolk Show in Saxmundham but I wouldn't have wanted to live in those times for a moment.

I had the idea for this book whilst driving home from a funeral. For a little while, it seemed like all the wonderful and weird characters that peppered my growing up were slipping away.

I suppose what I feared most was that the character of Saxmundham was disappearing with them. Nothing of the sort.

Young and new Saxmundhamers can be just as funny, just as kind, just as wonderful and weird.

This book became my attempt to try and capture stories that would otherwise be unheard. To build a mosaic that would depict Saxmundham, each person's story telling a small part of a bigger picture of the town.

My sincere and heartfelt gratitude goes to everyone who took the time to speak to me or to recommend someone else who might. I feel enormously lucky to have spent time with so many delightfully lovely and genuinely witty Saxmundham people.

Hugh Aldous b.1935

Hugh Aldous was born in Bury St Edmunds in 1935. His mother's family, the Longs, lived at Hurts Hall in Saxmundham and it was there that Hugh Aldous spent his infancy, alongside his sister Judith.

Hurts Hall had been owned by the Long family since 1700. After being accidentally burned down, it was rebuilt, to the building we see today, in 1893.

Hugh Aldous's grandfather, William Evelyn Long, was Squire Long and in 1914 was High Sheriff of Suffolk and, working with local government, helped to improve services in Saxmundham. Being Squire, he owned land in and around the town and employed many local agricultural workers, many of whom were also his tenants.

In 1939 when war broke out, Hugh Aldous and his sister were moved to the safety of Perthshire in Scotland to stay with their mother's uncle, Captain Bruce Vernon Wentworth. Their mother remained in Saxmundham where she worked for the WVS (the Woman's Voluntary Service).

"I remember Dall House by Loch Rannoch well. It was surrounded by mountains and lochs and beautiful scenery; the mountains were covered in snow most of the winter. We never heard a bomb the whole War. We lived there until we returned to Suffolk in 1947."

The siblings attended the local junior school in Scotland and went off to boarding schools in the south of England when they returned.

While the family was away, Hurts Hall was occupied and used as offices for the Army's 79th Armoured Division. Although it was likely that Winston Churchill visited the Hall when he came to Saxmundham, nearby Sternfield House was the usual meeting place for the Generals (including Field Marshall Montgomery and General Eisenhower) when they were preparing for the D-Day Allied invasion of Normandy for example.

When Hugh and Judith Aldous came back to Suffolk in 1947, the family moved back to Hurts Hall and lived there with the children's uncle, WG Long (known as Billy) and grandmother, Muriel Long.

In addition to managing Hurts Hall Farm and Wood Farm, adjacent to the Leiston Road, Billy Long worked as a solicitor in London. After he died in 1955, Hurts Hall was sold.

Hugh Aldous's sister, Judith, studied to be a nurse at Addenbrooke's in Cambridge, going on to Bible College in Swansea from where she went as a nursing missionary to northern Nigeria. She now lives in Australia.

Hugh Aldous's career included time spent working for a flooring and furnishing firm in London, a compass and binocular firm on Carlton Park and a farm machinery business in Friston. He continues to live in Saxmundham.

Marian Andrews b.1936

Being in a protected profession, Marian Andrews's father, Henry
James Turton, spent the Second World War in London. He worked
close to St Paul's Cathedral, printing the forged papers and fake
passports that were used by The Resistance. He received high praise
for his work from his superiors, 'for the book which you managed to
produce while the bombs were raining down'.

Marian Andrews attended the Henrietta Barnett Grammar
School in Hampstead Garden Suburb, but didn't stay on. When she
was 18, she became engaged to her first husband, Michael Cuming,
and they were married when she was 20.

Michael Cuming was part of the last intake for National Service,
and because he had a degree in physics, was offered a commission in
the Royal Navy. Marian Andrews embarked on life as a Navy wife
in married quarters, initially in Portsmouth, where the couple's first
daughter was born, then Culdrose in Cornwall and subsequently
Lossiemouth on the Moray Firth.

"Michael had two, 'pierhead jumps' during our marriage – that was
the expression that was used for being appointed to a ship at the last
minute – one to HMS Protector, the ice patrol ship in Antarctica
and one to HMS Belfast. Our second daughter arrived during the
HMS Belfast posting but I was staying with my parents in London."

The family was posted to Hong Kong in 1962, a very different
life, with plentiful help for an officer's wife;

"One of the other Naval wives was going back to the UK and I
was offered her job, working for a charity which ran playgrounds
for poor children. One of these was in Kowloon, which was an
extremely deprived area, and I worked there in the mornings, the
only European on the staff. I did pick up some Cantonese, but the
majority of staff spoke English."

On returning to the UK, Marian Andrews's husband was seconded
to the Fleet Air Arm and assigned a married quarter in Ruislip. He

was then posted to the US Navy base in Norfolk, Virginia, shortly after which the couple separated.

"My daughters and I moved back in with my parents and I spent 12 years on my own. Towards the end of that time, I took a job in local government and ended up working in the personnel department in Barking and Dagenham Council."

It was there that Marian Andrews met her second husband, Raymond Andrews, with whom she bought a house in Albion Street, Saxmundham, in 1980.

"We thought that it was a lovely town but were appalled by how many empty shops there were. We decided we could either throw the towel in and leave or try and do something about it.

Richard Crisp asked me to join the 'Say no to Tesco' campaign and as a result of that, I helped found CARA, The Chapel Area Residents' Association. A vacancy came up on the Town Council, which I stood for and didn't get, but did manage to be elected the following occasion."

Since then, Marian Andrews has chaired Saxmundham Town Council twice and now stands as one of the area's District Councillors, a position she has held for 11 years. She plans to retire before the election in 2015 when she will be moving to live near her youngest daughter near Manchester. Her eldest daughter lives in Melbourne, Australia.

Alan Barber b.1942

Alan Barber was 12 when he first went to sea with his father on a herring steam drifter out of Lowestoft.

After leaving school at 15 and studying for his licence at Lowestoft Maritime College, he signed up as a hand on steam drifters and went to Fleetwood where he spent three years working on trawlers.

Ready for adventure, Alan Barber heard about a job on what was known as a 'Fray Bentos', a vast refrigerated cargo ship that carried meat from Paraguay – a six month trip. With no immediate ties, (his mother died when he was 12 and his sister and father were settled) Alan Barber packed his kit bag and set off, hitching a ride on a tug to Tibury, where the refrigerated cargo ships docked. Instead the tug pulled in for the night in Greenwich.

"I checked in to the sailors' digs and was headed to the pub when I saw all these crowds of people. Turns out they were going to see Billy Smart's Circus. Well, there was a notice up wanting men to help pull down the circus tent after the closing show on Saturday, and because I knew how to splice and handle rope and wire, they took me on for that."

Alan Barber worked for Billy Smart's Circus for three years, first as a rigger, then as an elephant groom, responsible for taking care of five of the circus's twenty elephants at shows across the UK and at the winter quarters in Windsor.

"The elephants choose you; the trainer will take you in to meet them but they go to the person they want looking after them."

He returned home to Yoxford intending to head back to the circus but instead met his wife Carol Spatchett, a Saxmundham girl, with whom he set up home in the town and had two children, Paul and Hayley.

He continued to work on the trawlers out of Lowestoft, two weeks on and two days off, until the Common Fisheries Policy of the 1970s had its impact on the trade.

"There was nothing like Saxmundham on market day. When it was a sale day on a Wednesday, all the lads used to put their suits on and get on the train from Lowestoft and come into town. The High Street was packed with people and the pubs were open all day."

Mary Baskett b.1938

For more than a generation, Clarke's grocers and café was one of the most popular shops on Saxmundham High Street.

Mary Baskett's (nee Clarke) father started the business in the early 1930s.

"My grandfather, Charles, had been a saddlemaker in Saxmundham and my father, Claude Clarke, started the grocery business on the High Street. He was just getting the business going when he had to go off to the War."

With Claude Clarke away on military service, the running of the business fell to his wife Margery.

"Mum was too kind, really, she always wanted to help people out, so when Dad came back, the business wasn't in the best of shape!"

The Clarke family lived in two bedrooms above the shop and one living room to the rear. Both Mary and her sister Ann were born above the shop.

When Claude Clarke returned from the War, he made the bold move to open a Tea Garden at the back of the building with a handful of tables under an apple tree.

"At first there was just four or five tables at the back and we did tea and cakes. Soon, Dad decided that we'd give over our back room so that he could extend the Tea Garden into a restaurant offering hot meals. Mum was not very happy!"

Clarke's café proved enduringly popular and the lunches were a favourite amongst those who worked in the town.

"We used to do a roast lunch with two veg and a sweet every day. There'd be a lot of regulars amongst people who worked in the town. Mr Argent used to come in every day, for example, and have his lunch with three or four others."

The business, which was open six days a week, was hard work for all the family.

"I remember I used to love tennis but I could never go to tennis club after school because I had to help pack grocery boxes for delivery. At first we had a hand cart then I graduated to a trade bike and eventually we got a van.

It was hard work. You worked for 12 hours a day and the only time we had off was on bank holidays and Christmas. Our treat on bank holidays was to go to Yarmouth on the train."

When she was 15, Mary Baskett's father bought a house on Chapel Terrace on Rendham Road and the family was able to move out from the shop. Later, after she'd married, he had a bungalow built on Admiral Paton's land beside Fairfield House.

"It was lovely to be able to move out of the shop. My husband, Eric, was a postman from Kelsale. We were married in 1961 and we stayed living in Chapel Terrace when Mum and Dad went to live in the bungalow. My sister had also got married and moved away."

When Claude Clarke died in 1976, Mary Baskett and her husband took over the running of the business.

"It was just as hard work then, I'm not surprised that our son Carl didn't want to take the business on.

Sometimes it seems like we've gone full circle; there we were, packing up grocery orders for delivery and today, people are doing the same only the orders are being made online."

Sir Peter Batho, Bt b.1939
Lady Batho (Lucille) b.1945

As a small boy, Peter Batho's dream was to be a farmer.

"I wanted to farm from the age of about six, and was very lucky that my parents bought Park Farm in 1955. They bought it from Ivan Mann, who had lived here with his brother and mother. I remember watching my father sitting with Sam Flick going through the sale with Alice Brown, his secretary, taking notes."

Peter Batho was born in Welwyn, Hertfordshire and moved with his family to Ingatestone in 1947. The family moved to London in 1953 and all the school holidays were spent in Thorpeness.

"We spent every school holiday in Thorpe, not just the summer. In the winter, it was practically deserted."

Arthur Crisp, known as Ted, managed Park Farm, and his son John Crisp worked on the farm, on behalf of the Bathos, until 1959. The Batho family moved into the farm in 1961 and, after finishing school and attending Writtle Agricultural College, Peter Batho took over the job of cowman.

"We had a herd of 40 dairy cows then. Park Farm was originally 105 acres but we bought more here and there, when it became available, and today there are 300 acres of which 250 are usable. I took over the job of farm manager in 1963."

In 1966, Peter Batho married Lucille Williamson in Beccles. Her family lived in The White House, not far from Park Farm on Saxmundham's South Entrance.

"After school and a few months at Ipswich Civic College doing a secretarial course, I went to London for a bit. I came back to Saxmundham to work for my father, who was a solicitor and had a practice in the town."

J Noel Cooper and Williamson was an independent firm of solicitors with offices in Saxmundham Market Place. Lucille Williamson's father, Wilfrid, managed the practice until he retired in the 1970s.

"After we were married, we moved into Park Farm and Peter's

parents went to live at Carlton Hall.

I remember catching the train to Thorpeness Holt to play golf and to Aldeburgh for tennis. There seemed to be so many characters in the town then. Mr Proudfoot, who had a shop on the Market Place used always to go to the Carnival on stilts. Then there was Miss Turner, a sweet little lady and one of three sisters, who had a shop called The Green Shop, where Cards & Celebrations now is. She sold toys and gifts and it was always totally chaotic, with things falling off shelves! My brother and I loved spending our pocket money there."

Lucille and Peter Batho went on to have three sons, Rupert, Alexander and Hugh, and in the early 1980s, Peter Batho was elected to Saxmundham Town Council. In 1989 he became a Conservative member of Suffolk County Council where he served until 1993. He has been a District Councillor since 2003.

"I enjoyed the County Council enormously. I was particularly interested in County Farms which came about after WW1, to help people get started in farming. I chaired that committee while I was a member of the County Council. The trouble is, in the 1950s, a typical family farm was about 50 acres, whereas now you need at least 500 to make a viable living. Many of the largest farms in the region have upwards of 2,000 acres."

"I miss sale days in Saxmundham on alternate Wednesdays, of course, and I miss the town on a Saturday afternoon – many people used to work on Saturday mornings, so the only time to get out was on Saturday afternoon, the pavements were packed."

Freda Bibby b.1924

When Freda Bibby's family moved from Bigsby's Corner to Saxmundham when she was seven, she walked the whole way pushing her dolls in their pram.

"We had to move because the cottage we were in belonged to the Long Estate and they wanted it back."

When she was 14, she started work at Martin's, the women's and men's outfitters on Saxmundham High Street.

"We sold everything, hats, haberdashery, curtaining, cottons and other fabric as well as the ladies' and mens' clothes. Ladies were downstairs with millinery at the back and upstairs Mr Martin ran the men's department.

"My job was to take care of customers. There was one lady who used to come from Darsham on a pony and trap. I'd have to take roll after roll of material out for her to look at while the trap was parked on the High Street.

Every Monday the window was stripped and the girl who looked after it would do a new one afresh."

Freda Bibby (nee Burrows) married James at St John's church, Saxmundham when she was 19. He was batman to the Brigadier stationed locally and the couple met when he came in to the shop for cottons for the Brigadier's household. After they were married they lived with Freda Bibby's parents on Rendham Road.

"I went back to work after I was married until I fell pregnant with our daughter, Sheila. She was eight months old when my husband was sent Burma and four when he came back. She didn't know him and used to run straight to my father."

After demob, James Bibby got a job at the food office in Saxmundham, dealing with people's ration books and tokens. From there he went into local government.

"When the Blyth authority closed he went to work for Suffolk Coastal in Woodbridge.

After our daughter had got married, I was spending a lot of time on my own. My husband came in one day and said, 'get your coat – there's a job going at the cake shop in Woodbridge'. I really didn't want to go – told him I wouldn't do it and didn't even want to get out of the car when we got there, but I did and ended up working there for 19 and a half years until we both retired! It was the happiest time of my life."

Philip Bloomfield b.1950

Philip Bloomfield first discovered his love for photography when he was 18.

"The first camera I had was a cheap little cartridge-type; then I had a Zenit E and a Praktika MTL3, one of the ones you would wind on between shots with 35mm film. When I was able to, I got a good quality Olympus. I was a self-taught amateur, I read a lot and learnt as I went along."

In the 1980s, Saxmundham Carnival was sponsored by Ipswich Building Society.

"I went in and enquired at their office at the end of Saxmundham High Street and they made me official photographer for the Carnival. We'd hang sheets with copies of the pictures in the window of the shop and people would order the prints they wanted."

Saxmundham Carnival had played a big part in the annual life of the life of the town since the early 20th century. The parade, led by a marching band, followed by lines of floats and individuals in fancy dress, went from Flicks saleground (where Waitrose supermarket now is) along the High Street to Carlton Park. Philip Bloomfield used to climb up the railway embankment near the bridge to get an overhead shot of the parade going past and then run to the Park so that he was in time for the parade's arrival. Hundreds would take part.

"The Carnival Princess Selection Dances at the Market Hall were great nights. The only trouble was that by 9 o'clock, the room was so thick with smoke, photography was out of the window!"

Philip Bloomfield also photographed other well-known local events including the Lambfair, Henham Steam Rally and Yoxford Oxfair.

His parents, who had met in Italy during the War, moved in with his father's family at 'The Villas', a pair of semi-detatched cottages at the rear of the building now occupied by Flicks, across a small bridge over the Fromus. The family lived there for three years, during which time Philip Bloomfield and his brother, Alf, were born. They them moved to Leiston Airfield, where his father was stationed, before returning to Saxmundham.

Philip Bloomfield's father left the family when Philip was seven, leaving his mother to bring up three boys on her own in a house in Park Avenue.

"Things were very tough in those days. You used to fix everything. I remember my Mum darning our socks. All three of us boys learnt to cook and sew at a very early age."

After school, he worked at Street Farm, and also helped to look after the cattle at Park Farm and Brook Farm.

"There was a lot of work about in the early 1970s and I moved to a job at Brett Brothers in Friston. They were mechanical engineers which I really enjoyed because I'd always been mechanically minded.

After that, I went on to work for AJ Mew's scrap metal merchants in Rendham Road; it was really hard work but I learnt to drive a crane. When Stephen Mew took over, he put me through driving lessons because, even though I'd been driving tractors for years, I'd never got a car licence. I went for my test in Lowestoft and passed first time then came straight back to work – I went from driving a Mini to a 23 ton crane in one afternoon!"

AJ Mew was one of the

busiest scrap merchants in the area.

"We used to do a lot of work for Garretts in Leiston, moving heavy stuff, we even used to break up old trawlers."

When AJ Mew closed, Phil Bloomfield worked at Sizewell B for three years and then went on to Notcutts in Pettistree working in dispatch and in the tree nursery.

He has one son from his marriage to Rosalyn who died in 2003.

Olive Bolton b.1935

On Olive Bolton's ninth birthday, her mother took her to buy a special party dress. The family lived in Plaistow, near the docks in London's East End, and her father was away serving in the War.

"We'd bought my dress and were on our way home. Mum and I got off the bus and walked towards the house but it was gone! We were very lucky that we were out when the bomb landed, but the remains of the house were just hanging there, everything we owned had gone."

Olive Bolton and her mother were evacuated to distant relatives in West Suffolk, a village called Whatfield near Hadleigh. "I immediately fell in love with Suffolk, its space and fields and meadows."

She and her mother, and recently demobbed father, returned to London after the War to live with her grandmother. She trained as a nurse and worked at Charing Cross Hospital in casualty.

Olive was married to John Bolton shortly after her 22nd birthday. His job as a railway engineer took them across the country, starting at Crewe then Derby, Plymouth and Buckinghamshire. "Our daughter Penny came along quite quickly and very soon we had three children under four years; Penny, Simon and Guy. It meant that I didn't work as a nurse for a while!"

By the time the children were settled at school and Guy's health stabilised, Olive Bolton enrolled at the Sidney Webb College, studying two evenings a week and one weekend a month for four years for a Certificate in Teaching.

"John got a job in Norwich and we needed to be near a train station to get Guy back and forth to Great Ormond Street. When I first came to Saxmundham, I loved it because of the beautiful countryside plus there were lots of shops and it was close to the coast. There wasn't much building going on in the town in those days except for the American estate.

We used to like going to Clarke's on the High Street for lunch, it was a bit like a deli with a café at the back – where Angel's beauticians is now."

Olive Bolton began working as a supply teacher at the primary school in Dennington. When the education system changed from two-tier to three-tier in the 1970s, and resulted in the creation of middle schools, she took a job at Leiston Middle School as a second year (today's Year 6) class teacher.

"I especially enjoyed arts and crafts and loved working with children in that age group. I do a lot of craft work with our grandchildren now."

Olive and John Bolton live at Brook Cottage, a house with a large and varied history. It has been, over the years, a school for 'Young Gentlemen', home to a local solicitor and was originally part of Brook Farm, in the days when it was a dairy farm rather than a housing estate.

"Surprisingly, the Brook Farm estate hasn't made too much difference to us, although we did lose a bit of garden. What made the most difference was the building of the A12 bypass. When the A12 ran through the centre of town, it sometimes seemed impossible to get out of our gate there was so much traffic. The bypass made a big difference to that, but had a detrimental effect to many of the businesses on the

high street."

Olive Bolton was one of the original stewards at Saxmundham Museum and co-founder of CARA, a resident's association that took elderly people for a monthly outing for tea and crafts at the Chapel School Rooms.

"Saxmundham has changed completely over the last 40 years but I still wouldn't want to live anywhere else."

Tony Brown b.1934

Tony Brown is the fourth of nine children, born in Middleton where his father worked as a steamroller driver.

"We were in Middleton until I was 13. Then the farmer decided that he wanted the cottage back and we all had to move. Dad found work in Friston so we went there, but then the Council took over that property and we had to move again. They put us in the hospital building on Leiston Aerodrome – it sounds very disruptive but it was the first time we'd had a flush toilet and the first time I'd had a room of my own. It was marvellous."

When he was 15, Tony Brown left school and started work on a farm at East Green, Kelsale.

"I left school on the Friday and started work on the Saturday morning. At first I used to cycle from the airfield and then I took lodgings at Kelsale. I wanted to join the air force as an air force policeman, like my eldest brother, but I had a perforated eardrum so they didn't want me, so I stayed on the farm."

When he was 22, Tony Brown married Pauline Mann from Knodishall, and the couple moved into a cottage at Rubblestone Farm, East Green. They went on to have three children; Stephen, David and Diana.

"The thing is, I've always wanted to get on. I saw a job advertised for a Head Pigman in Albury, Hertfordshire, working for Prince Frederick von Prussia. In the morning, you'd have to say 'Good Morning, your Highness,' and call him 'Sir' after that. But he was a lovely man. He had one boar and a couple of dozen sows.

One day, I was sitting aback one of the sows having a ride round the orchard when Princess Brigid came out and asked what I was doing. She loved animals and hopped on behind me to ride around too!"

After a year, Prince Frederick decided that he wasn't after all going to extend his herd so Tony Brown and his family moved back to

Kelsale, working again for Mr Easey.

"I saw the job of Farm Manager advertised for Mr Marks at Kelsale and I thought, why shouldn't I give that a go? So I applied and got the job and we moved to a bungalow on the farm. He had 110 acres with about 80 sows and two bulls.

The boars were Large Whites – the big ones with the ears that stand up – they're very intelligent creatures and they get to know you. You've got to treat them with respect. Well, we'd had this salesman come to the farm and he'd been teasing the boar and I could see the boar was riled. When I opened the pen later to let him out, he charged at me and ripped my leg open with his tusks. They took me to the house and laid me down until the doctor came and gave me six aspirins and a glass of whiskey! It's a wonder that didn't finish me off! I've still got a huge scar on my leg, 60 years later!"

Tony Brown spent four years working as Farm Manager for Mr Marks at Kelsale.

"Then the Governor dropped dead and the family wanted the property so we had to move on. We went to Beaumont Cottages in Kelsale."

In 1965, having been a volunteer with St John's Ambulance for around six years, Tony Brown joined the Ambulance Service at the newly-built ambulance station on Seaman Avenue, Saxmundham. He was to stay working there for 14 years.

"It was a wonderful job, we used to be called out all over – as far as Bury. The rules were that you must be the 'nearest available' ambulance. When the unions started telling us to work to rule and so on, I decided I'd had enough."

Having worked as a bearer for various local funeral services over the years, Tony Brown knew what to expect when he started his own funeral business in 1979.

"I'd been helping out at Leiston Funeral Services for some time and they gave me a lot of advice. At first, I used to hire Ashford's hearse but I had a wonderful bank manager by the name of Mr Studd at Barclays and when I'd been going about two years, he arranged for me to borrow the money to buy my own hearse. It wouldn't happen now!"

After someone complained about Tony Brown running his business from home in Kelsale, he started looking for premises in Saxmundham.

"The old stone mason's, Smyths, on New Cut had been put on the market and I arranged to buy that. We had to pull everything down and start afresh. I couldn't afford a digger so I dug all the footings myself with a garden spade!"

Tony Brown's Funeral Directors is one of the most successful in the area. It is also a pioneer of green burials with a 77 acre green burial site at Farnham attracting 'residents' from all over the UK.

"I went 13 years without a day off and was on call for all that time! I enjoyed it, it's a way of helping people. If I were 10 years younger, I'd do it every day if I could. I've done 9,000 funerals in 35 years.

When I was younger, we'd always come into Sax for sale day. At Middleton, I'd breed rabbits to sell, but you used to come in just for the sake of it. It was a wonderful time!"

Eric Burrows b.1932

Eric Burrows was born in the middle of the three workhouse cottages that once stood opposite what are now Ensors Accountants offices on Rendham Road.

As a boy he was a keen fisherman, catching roach and other tiddlers from Saxmundham's many ponds. He's been known as 'Tiddler' ever since.

"We used to fish in the corner pond and the 12 acre pond that were both the other side of where the bypass now is. One day, I was down at Collins's pond* I fell in – one of my step brothers pulled me out but they said that I was going down for the third time!"

Eric Burrows was a pupil at Saxmundham Primary School on Fairfield Road. Before the school employed a cook, "Betty Miller and her mum", the children used to run home for lunch and back again.

"I was quite naughty in those days but I never got the cane. Our neighbour, Mrs Dolby used to shout out to Mother, 'call Eric to get the frog out of my drain!' so I'd go round and get the frog out and take it away in my bucket and Mrs Dolby would give me sixpence. If I was lucky, I'd get another sixpence for getting it out again after I'd put it back in the drain the next day!

There were some wonderful times. I remember lamb sale day which was once a year in the spring. It was quite an event, with the shepherd's driving the lambs along the road from Kelsale and Benhall. Some came in trucks, but most, they just came along the road. Mr Flick would do the sale. That's why they call it Lambsale Meadow where the doctors' is now."

Eric Burrows started work at 14 with Mr Hall at Hill House Farm in Benhall. He then went on to be second cowman on Park Farm, Saxmundham for Maurice Batho.

When the workhouse cottages were demolished, Eric Burrows' family moved to a new house in Saxon Road. Unfortunately, his mother didn't get to enjoy the new home for long. She died as a result of a bad fall whilst out collecting funds for the Royal British Legion.

In 1955, he married Jean (nee Watling). They have two sons, Adrian and Russell.

"We used to have a reserved 'cuddle seat' at the Picture House. It was a great place until it rained because the tin roof made it sound like you were under fire!"

Eric Burrows began his career as a builder with Roadworks Ltd of Ipswich.

"They used to pick us up on a truck with a shack on the back and we'd ride on that to the site. Then I went to Costains and we built the aircraft shelters at Bentwaters and the Colchester and Ipswich bypasses."

Eric Burrows played for Saxmundham Football Club for 15 years. He was also secretary of the Saltwater Section of Saxmundham Angling Club.

"There was a wonderful social side to the clubs. We had dances on all special occasions, led by Dennis Page and Kay Goddard and later, we used to go to their dances wherever they were on a Saturday night.

We knew everyone in Sax in the old days."

Collins's Pond is behind the Fire Station on Seaman Avenue.

Harry Butcher b.1925 *(sitting)*
Chris Butcher b.1961 *(standing)*

In June 2014, Chris Butcher had tea with Her Majesty the Queen at a Garden Party to which he was invited in gratitude for the thousands of pounds that he's raised for charity.

Committed Salvationists, Chris Butcher and his father Harry, who was unfortunately too frail to make the trip to the Palace, are well known around Saxmundham for the collections that they make in the town's pubs every Friday night, and at local events.

Harry Butcher was born in Friston. He served in the Second World War in the Worcestershire regiment, rather than the local Royal Anglians, "They'd lost too many of their men, we had to fill in for them." He served in France and Germany.

After the War, Harry Butcher settled in Station Approach, Saxmundham with his wife Ethel. He looked after the Gannon Rooms, managing bookings and caretaking and was a caretaker at Saxmundham Primary and Middle Schools. He was also a well-known lollipop man, helping pupils across North Entrance, outside the old doctor's surgery.

In 1958, the family moved to one of the 'new' houses on Saxon Road and were soon joined by sons Conrad and Christopher.

Ethel Butcher ran the Salvation Army Sunday School in Saxmundham for more than 50 years. She had been bought up as an active member of the Salvation Army, although it wasn't until 1968, that Harry Butcher joined too.

Today, the Butchers are the only Salvation Army family in Saxmundham, but many others attend their Sunday evening worship at the Chapel, with the Minister coming from Woodbridge.

Chris Butcher has taken over the hosting of a weekly fellowship at their home, "We get together for a cup of tea and a sandwich, sing and pray together. It's a good way of meeting people and making friends. Everyone's welcome."

Chris Butcher was bought up in the Salvation Army and

attended Saxmundham Primary School and Ashley Downs school in Lowestoft. He enjoys his weekly trips to the pubs, "You meet all sorts of people. You find that people often give you money when you're on the way out because they feel a bit guilty about ignoring you when you've come in!"

Howard Cadman b.1935

Howard Cadman was born in Great Glemham where his mother ran the village shop.

"Mother had inherited the General Stores and Post Office. It was a busy life – she used to do telegrams too and originally went about on a motorbike. Father worked on the railway all his life. There were five of us children, four boys and one girl."

Just before Howard Cadman turned eight, the family sold the business and moved to Chantry Road in Saxmundham. It was a large house with a spacious back garden.

"I went to the Primary School in Fairfield Road and before there was a cook, we used to go down the road to Oddfellows Hall and have our dinner there, of course some of us used to run off into town too!"

The Oddfellows is a non-political, non-denominational friendly society that was founded in 1810. Its aims are 'making friends and helping people'.

The Oddfellows' Hall in Fairfield Road, Saxmundham, is now a private house.

Before he left school, Howard Cadman was responsible for raising the family's hens.

"There was a shed at the back of the house that Mother let out as a carpentry shop. I kept 60 or 70 chickens in the loft – I was 12 or 13, I suppose. Mother used to pack the eggs up and the man would come and collect them. We kept a couple of pigs too – there's a story."

Howard Cadman's father was biking home to Saxmundham from Snape Maltings where he'd been overseeing the delivery of a train load of grain.

"Mr Crisp had had a sow die and he asked Father if we could take care of a couple or three little piglets. He tucked them up in the box on the back of his bike with some sandbags so that they felt secure and when they were settled, Father set off home.

Well, he thought he could hear a binder going and wondered if there was a rabbit to be had. He was a hell of a shot with a catapult. He got his rabbit and arrived home in Chantry Road with that and the piglets. We got the piglets going, bottle fed them and bought them up. In the end one weighed 22 stone and the other nearly 21!"

When he was 15, Howard Cadman started work for William Salter at Hill Farm, Saxmundham, starting as a general labourer.

"I'd help Billy Bloss the ploughman; do some milking; a bit of everything really. There was a terrible fire one day in the thatched barn It was a very hot day, everything was completely dry. It must have been started by a spark from the tractor engine. It went up so quickly you wouldn't believe. I ran up to the house to get them to call the fire brigade and there was Mrs Salter playing cards. There'd been a barrel of paraffin that we didn't find until days later – it had been blown 50 yards across the field. Incredibly, we only lost one chicken!

By the time I was 17 or 18, I was the only one left on the estate. The Salters had had a lovely big house built by Reeds and there was about 4 acres there. I finished off with a bit of ploughing and milking the home cow. Like a lot of farm women, Mrs Salter used to make cream and butter."

When William Salter died, the farm tenancy went back to the Hollond Estate at Benhall. Howard Cadman went to work at Brook Farm for Mr Hicks.

"He had a lovely herd of Ayreshire milkers as well as chickens and some pigs. I did a bit of everything."

Howard Cadman married Saxmundham girl Pauline Holland in 1963. Although they'd been at primary school together, Pauline Holland had gone on to the Grammar School at Leiston using one of the bicycles that the Local Authority issued to children that lived furthest from the school.

"When the weather was bad, we did take the bus but of course then you had to find the bus fare!"

Howard and Pauline Cadman moved to Albion Street when they were first married and, after about five years, on to one of the then new bungalows at the top of Saxon Road.

At that time, before the building of the housing estate, Howard Cadman could walk through the hedge at the bottom of his garden and be on a meadow where he could start herding the cows.

Pauline Cadman worked as a seamstress making curtains and loose covers, including for Ashfords the department store. She also worked at the desk at Harcourt's butchers. With the financial pressures of married life, Howard Cadman made the decision to move on from farm work.

"I loved being on the farm but it was never well paid. I joined Roadworks Ltd, alongside some of my friends from Saxmundham.

Howard Cadman wins the 220yd race at Fram Gala in 1948. The handicap system meant that he had started from the back row of the lineup.

We went all over the place and I ended up being there to build Sizewell B power station.

It was hard work, very long hours but very interesting, every different nationality. I remember when the dome was lifted in to place – it was extraordinary. They used one of the biggest cranes in Europe and it fitted like a glove."

Howard Cadman stayed in the construction industry across Suffolk until his retirement, working at, amongst other sites, RAF Woodbridge, Felixstowe Docks and the new A14.

Richard Crisp b.1943

Richard Crisp knew from when he was a small boy that he would one day take over the family printers and stationers on Saxmundham High Street.

"Crisp's was started by my great grandfather, Henry Buxton Crisp in 1867, when the core business was a printing works. He retired in 1904 to be succeeded by his son, Henry George Crisp, who in turn passed the business to his son, Arthur Henry Crisp, my father."

Richard Crisp's parents moved to South Entrance when they got married and that is where Richard Crisp spent his childhood. His grandparents continued to live in the house adjoining the shop.

"I went away to board at Culford School near Bury St Edmunds but I really enjoyed being in Saxmundham in the holidays, playing on the layers and up at Carlton."

At 17, Richard Crisp began his business and retail training in Chelmsford. He continued his training London where he worked in The Times Bookshop in Wigmore Street, amongst other places, living in the capital for four and a half years.

"After London, I went travelling; skiing in Norway, then travelled through East Germany, Switzerland, Italy, Greece, then Istanbul before taking the train home via Paris. I wanted to pack as much in as I could because I knew that I'd go on to be based back in Saxmundham running the business."

In 1966, Richard Crisp joined his father in the business which was, at the time, primarily a letterpress printers employing five people and producing business and personal stationery, posters, cards and an enduringly popular timetable showing local trains and buses.

There were four further employees in the shop selling pens, stationery goods and books.

Richard Crisp married Vivienne (whose parents had started the popular Aldringham Craft Market) in 1969 and the couple moved to Dorley's Corner. They went on to have three children.

"The print works finally closed in 1971 when it ceased to be competitive. In 1974, I made the decision to expand into books and children's books and eventually converted rooms that had previously been part of the house into more retail space."

In 1977, he expanded the business to include cards, toys, art materials and a very popular photo processing department.

"Saxmundham was different in those days because you knew everyone, in fact people that you didn't know stood out. It meant that you had a special connection with your customers – you could get the same person coming in for the same magazine every week for 40 years!"

After selling the business upon his retirement in 2007, Richard Crisp focussed his attentions on the formation of Saxmundham Museum (which contains a replica of the original Crisp's shop front and a tableau of the printing process).

"The Museum was born out of the Local History Society. I worked together with Helen Revell to get it started, although Gary Eves and John Shove were also instrumental. Tony Flick bought the building and leased it to us and people were incredibly generous, donating artifacts and fascinating pieces of local history."

In addition to continuing work as Chairman of Saxmundham Museum, Richard Crisp is a trustee of the charity STOW, a founder member of the St John Drama Group and Chair of the Saxmundham Local History Society.

"Saxmundham is an incredibly special place. It may not have a castle or a seaside, but it does have a heart."

Lyla Edmunds b.1919

Lyla Edmunds was born in Woodbridge in 1919, one of ten children; eight boys and two girls. Her father was a tailor as his parents had been before him.

Like many girls of her age, Lyla Edmunds entered service at 14; "it was hard, they always gave us youngsters the dirty jobs".

Once in Saxmundham, she worked as a cook and housekeeper at Mr and Mrs Russell's school in Rendham Road, a small private school for children whose parents worked abroad. She went on to work for many of the areas best known families including Lord and Lady Sinclair and Dr John Ryder Richardson.

Her husband Chris was in the Royal Air Force and was posted to Africa just three weeks after their marriage. He was sent home soon after, having contracted malaria, "you wouldn't recognise him, he'd lost so much weight and looked so ill".

Chris Edmunds found it difficult to settle after leaving the RAF once the war was over and worked variously as a cowman, for the electricity board, and finally as a chimney sweep.

The couple raised two daughters; Pauline and Mary, and three grandchildren, Christopher, Tim and Sally Ann Newson.

"Saxmundham was so busy in those days, the High Street was always full of people, there were even three sweet shops! I miss the old Saxmundham."

Peter Emsden b.1958

Ever since he was a small boy, Peter Emsden's ambition was to be in charge of his own ship.

"My uncle Roger used to come and see me when he was home from the lightships and he'd tell me stories of life at sea and give me models and things that he'd made while he was away – boats and tiny figures made out of shells."

Although Peter Emsden was born at the Phyllis Memorial in Melton, he came home to The Angel pub in Saxmundham where his parents, Peter and Mona, were tenant landlords.

The Angel, a 16th century Grade II listed coaching inn, was in Saxmundham Market Place, with its yard on north end of the High Street. It was a large pub, with stables, which in 1887 was described in an advertisement as a 'Commercial Hotel, Livery and Bait Stables - Every accommodation for Families and Commercial Gentlemen'.

"You could see it was an old pub, there were low beams and uneven floors. It was a big place, we had 14 rooms and the stables next door. People always tell me that they remember sawdust on the floor but actually it was sand – I remember my Dad sieving it in the morning while Mum scrubbed the benches."

It wasn't always easy for a child living above a pub in the 1960s. The jukebox music was loud and, in those days, almost everyone smoked.

"I had bad asthma, used to miss whole terms of school. I'd be at home, and someone would open the door to the stairs and all the smoke from the bar would rush upstairs."

The Angel was a Tolly Cobbold pub that had been sold to John Cobbold Jnr in 1921. By the 1970s, the brewer decided that one of their two pubs in Saxmundham had to go. It was either The Angel or the Refresh (later known as The Railway) and they chose The Angel. It was closed down and demolished in 1976 to make way for the offices and flats that now make up Angel Yard.

After school in Saxmundham and Leiston, Peter Emsden started work as an apprentice carpenter with Meadows Brothers of Friston but soon realised that it wasn't the career for him.

"Me and my friend Stephen Buzzard, we got on the train to London to the Merchant Navy office. We were about 16, I suppose. They took all our details but we never did hear anything. In the end, I went up to Lowestoft and got a job on the trawler fleet. Your first trip is an observation trip and then you become a 'deckie learner' it was tough work."

Peter Emsden learnt his trade on the fishing vessels, attending Lowestoft Maritime College to study for his Mates Certificate. He often helped out behind the bar at The Angel when he was home. It was in the mid-1980s that he found himself in the Cooper's Dip, chatting to Duncan McNichol.

"He was chief officer on a ship called Kommandor Therese and he was looking for a Duty Support Officer. A few weeks later there was a knock at the door and he was there asking me if I could join the ship at Great Yarmouth. I started off as an AB." (AB = Able Seaman)

The posting provided the introduction to working on DP, or Dynamic Positioning vessels. These are the ships that are designed to be able to maintain their position to within centimetres without anchors and are used as chiefly as dive support vessels, as a base for ROVs (Remotely Operated Vehicles), to lay pipelines and retrieve wreckage.

"I was off Sharja in the Arabian Gulf in 1988 on a vessel called the DSV Eastern Installer as one of the two 2nd Officer DPOs (DP Operators). We operated out of Sharjah in the UAE and worked at the Fereydoon and Rashadat oil fields clearing debris of platforms that the Americans had recently blown up from the seabed. It was still classed as a war zone so we got extra pay as soon as we entered Iranian waters."

In 2001, the Eastern Installer, by then called the Balmoral Sea, was in New Orleans when a fire broke out in her engine room.

The fire brigade was called and all hands evacuated while the fire brigade began filling the ship with water. "Unfortunately, the bilge pumps weren't running and the ship capsized! She was a write-off and scrapped, without doubt there would of have been a substantial insurance payout!"

In 1999, Peter Emsden fulfilled his childhood ambition and, after further studying, was awarded his Master's Certificate.

In 2011, he spent six months in Pusan in South Korea overseeing the construction of the Gulmar Atlantis, the 116 metres long Dive Support Vessel that would be under his command.

"I oversaw the build and the sea trials. She was designed and certified to carry a maximum 120 persons; the number could be made up of officers, crew, client reps and divers. The biggest complement that she carried when I commanded her was 118 and I was the only Brit on board. She took me to jobs in the Antarctic and all over the world.

I'd met my wife Fran in 2002. I was working out of the Gulf of Mexico and the cook was a Canadian who lived in the Philippines. It turned out that his wife was Fran's cousin."

Fran and Peter Emsden married in 2011 (he has three grown-up sons from his first marriage). After six months or so she began to find Peter's three-month absences too hard and he took a job with Seacorps working out of Yarmouth.

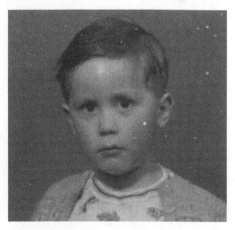

"We service the gas rigs in the southern North Sea. There are only 12 crew but we get home more often!"

Bernard Everett b.1936

Bernard Everett and his sister Maureen (Godfrey) were born in Saxmundham in Gas Works House, where the Police Station is now.

Bernard Everett's father was a gas fitter in the nearby gas works and he has early memories of going round the town with his father on a Saturday morning to change the mantles and clean the mirrors in the street lights.

His was a war-time childhood, when all the local men were either away or in the Home Guard. He started at Saxmundham Primary when he was four.

"When the sirens went off, we all had to go into the shelters with a book to read and we had to recite our times tables".

He remembers bombs landing in Saxmundham on 'our sweet shop' next door to Wells' hardware shop as well as on the cricket pitch on the layers.

Bernard Everett became a gas fitter himself after an apprenticeship in Leiston but four days after he qualified he started two year's National Service.

He worked at Sizewell for 33 years and was a keen footballer, playing in goal for Saxmundham Sports Club. After early retirement he became referee and manager for the Saxmundham Youth Club football team.

Bernard Everett now lives in Halesworth but recalls growing up in a more self-sufficient town. He said, "Saxmundham had its own brewery, saw mill and three bakers as well as the gas works".

Brenda Ferguson b.1940

Brenda Ferguson's family, the Smiths, came to Saxmundham from Loudham in 1952, when her father took up employment with Squire Long at Hurts Hall.

"We lived in Church Lodge, at the end of the drive to the Hall, and as children, we had freedom to roam all over the estate. We knew where to look for nesting birds, wild fruit, nuts and wild flowers and at Easter, we used to pick primroses and Lent lilies to decorate the church.

I used to sing in the church choir when Rev Moyle was rector and the organ had to be pumped by hand! I remember our first Christmas in Saxmundham because Mrs Aldous, the Squire's sister, organised a lovely party for the children of all of the estate workers."

Brenda Ferguson joined Saxmundham Primary School in Fairfield Road where, in addition to the three 'Rs', "we girls had a good grounding in cookery and sewing while the boys did woodwork and gardening. Country dancing was held in the quadrangle with the music provided by an ancient wind-up gramophone or Mr Foster on his violin!"

When she was 21, Brenda Ferguson's parents became landlords of the Railway Inn, next to Saxmundham Station.

"My parents were licensees at the Railway for 16 years and I used to help out working behind the bar and so on. This was in the last few years of steam trains which used to stop to fill up with water at Saxmundham."

The pub had been built as a refreshment house for the men building the railway and was known locally as 'The Fresh' for many years.

"When we first moved in, I used to get woken up by the milk train coming through in the early hours of the morning. We soon got used to them and I never heard the trains at all."

Brenda Ferguson left Saxmundham Primary School when she was 15 and went to work at the Pye factory in Leiston.

"I used to bike to work, with other girls from Saxmundham, and we reckoned to get to Leiston Works in ten minutes! While I was there, I went to evening classes to learn shorthand and typing. I then worked at the office for Ashfords in Saxmundham High Street.

"When I was 17 and a half, I made the decision to broaden my horizons and joined the Women's Royal Naval Service (WRNS). I had an uncle who'd been in the Navy for 35 years and I used to love his tales of life at sea. Also, I wanted to prove my father wrong because he said I'd never do it!"

When Brenda Ferguson had completed her basic training at Burghfield and Plymouth, she qualified as a Switchboard Operator and was posted to a Royal Naval Air Station in Northern Ireland followed by one in Scotland.

"I really enjoyed my time in the WRNS, seeing new places and meeting new people. Best of all, I met my husband, Ian!"

They were married in St John's, Saxmundham in 1960 and Ian Ferguson continued his service with the Royal Navy for a further 22 years.

"I worked at the Saxmundham Telephone Exchange until our first son, Duncan, was born. Then we went to Malta where Ian was stationed, which was fascinating. Our second son, Craig was born when we were back in Saxmundham."

As well as being Akela to the Saxmundham Cubs, Brenda Ferguson was a keen member of Saxmundham Ladies' Football Team, a very successful side with a large number of supporters. Her father was a referee.

"I loved growing up in Saxmundham, everything we needed was here. The highlight of the week was Wednesday, market day, when people from surrounding villages came in to shop. I used to love watching all the cows, pigs, sheep, rabbits and chickens being unloaded. On one occasion I remember, one of the bullocks made a bid for freedom and took off along the river bed towards Sternfield!"

Saxmundham Ladies Football Team 1956 season
Back row: L-R **? Brenda Ferguson**, Mary Smith, Diana Mann, Judy Chesterfield,
Christine Matterson
Front row: L-R Joy Smith, Audrey Clow, Dilys Kitson, ? , Gina Denny

John Feveyear b.1933

It's likely that only an enthusiast would be aware that there are two lawn bowls clubs in Saxmundham; Saxmundham Town and Saxmundham Sports.

John Feveyear now plays for Saxmundham Sports but has been a member of both.

"I've been playing for 29 years and I started by accident. I bumped into Eve Evans when I was out for a walk one day and she said, why didn't I come up to the club and have a look and a cup of tea? The next thing I knew, she'd arranged for me to borrow some balls and had signed me up for a match that afternoon! I don't think I was very good but I kept playing!"

Saxmundham Sports is based at Carlton Park and is renowned for having one of the best greens in the country. Saxmundham Town is a smaller club, based on land east of the High Street.

"I enjoy my bowls and my line dancing and I sing in the Rabble Chorus in the Gannon Rooms every Thursday. I don't want to sit around in front of the TV just because I'm retired."

John Feveyear was born in Wilby although the family moved to Brundish when he was still a young child. He had four brothers and one sister.

"My dad was a bricklayer and I wanted to be a carpenter but he said that it would be too expensive getting the tools and so on, so when I left school at 14, I started working on the land."

At 18, John Feveyear began his National Service based at Bury St Edmunds.

"We went all over; Trieste, Wildberg, Bielefeld. I was batman to a second lieutenant and a wireless operator. I was one of those that never minded looking after clothes and boots – I always hang my own things up at the end of the day."

After National Service, John Feveyear worked on a building site. He met his wife, June Smith, at the cinema in Framlingham. At the time she was working at Martins in Saxmundham High Street. They went on to have four sons.

"I'd been working at Cranes in Ipswich for a while and then I got the offer of a job in the stores at Sizewell A – it was being built at the time. It was really interesting work, even though I tended to do the night shift.

I was offered a permanent contract with CEGB and made up to Plant Attendant and finally ended up as a Plant Operator in the fuelling department. We used to do one month there and one month at the pond doing cooling elements. It was remote control, obviously, in a separate room because the radiation was so high. I ended up at Sizewell for 28 years.

"I was offered early retirement when I was 59. My wife was working at Somerfield at the time and two days after I retired, one of her colleagues got in touch to say that they were looking for someone to buff the floors. Eventually I agreed; it meant working from 6 to 8 every morning and I ended up doing it until I was 73!"

In the end, his sons persuaded John Feveyear to retire fully. His wife died in 2006 and his son Glenn in 2013.

Josephine Firman b.1928

After she'd left school at 14, Josephine Firman worked as an usherette at Saxmundham Picture House.

"We had a dark red uniform with braiding and a little hat. The Picture House was always full in those days because there were so many soldiers about. When there was an air raid, a siren went off and a warning used to come up on screen asking people to leave but I can't remember anyone going – they all wanted to get their money's worth!"

When she was 15, she started work as a nursemaid looking after twin baby boys for the Greenacre family in Yoxford. It was a live-in position.

"I used to get one half day off a week and would cycle home to Saxmundham, making sure that I was back in time to do the children's breakfasts the next morning."

Josephine Firman was born in Kesgrave and moved with her family to Saxmundham when she was six. She had two brothers and one sister. Her father was a post office engineer and came to Saxmundham to work in the depot at the north end of the High Street.

"My dad was on call virtually 24 hours a day during the War. They were handling calls from the army and so on. It took priority over everything. They couldn't join up, of course, and they weren't even meant to join the Home Guard, although they did start a small Home Guard unit of their own.

I was with the Greenacre family in Southwold when the news came through that war ended. I don't remember much about it except that everyone in the street seemed to be drunk!"

When the Greenacre twins went to boarding school, Josephine Firman moved to Carlton Rookery to take care of three children from the Sawday family.

"The family was very nice but in the end I just wanted to be at home."

She married her husband John when she was 24 and they have one son, Andrew.

"I'd been at school with John but I hadn't liked him much then! When we first got married, he worked at the sawmill on St John's Road but then he got a job at Fishers and worked alongside Mr Fisher and then Gary Smith until he retired. John died six years ago, just a few months before what would have been our 60th wedding anniversary."

When her son was school age, Josephine Firman started work for Dr John Ryder Richardson at Westhill on Rendham Road.

"I think I ended up working for Dr John for nearly 40 years, looking after the children, doing housework and so on. It was lovely."

John Fisher b.1947

The Phyllis Memorial was a maternity home just outside Melton in the building currently occupied by Melton Day Nursery. It was to here that Bernard Fisher cycled to see his wife, Hazel, and new son in 1947, after shutting up shop for the day in Saxmundham.

John Fisher lived above Fishers ironmongers with his family until they moved to Knodishall when he was eight, by which time he had a younger brother and sister. He attended Saxmundham Primary School on Fairfield Road and then Leiston Grammar School.

"Dad would bring us in with him in the mornings when he came to open the shop. After school, we'd wait around there until closing time. When I got into the Grammar School, I used to bike there from Knodishall and continued to do so when we'd moved to Manor Gardens in Sax."

After finishing school, John went to Queen Mary College, University of London to study Chemistry, although he changed to Maths during his first year. In the holidays, he took jobs monitoring radiation at the District Survey Lab at Sizewell A, and worked on a local farm. Towards the end of his course, he took a summer job as a London bus conductor and continued this work until he'd completed his time at university.

"I stayed on until January to re-take some modules on my course and continued to work throughout that time, saving up so that I could go travelling."

Having completed his degree, John went to Victoria station to request, 'A single to Istanbul, please.'

"I wanted to see India and Ceylon – my father had spoken about being in Ceylon during the War. It was possible in those days to buy a ticket to Istanbul then to get the proceeding tickets as you went along. It was fascinating."

In the summer after he returned, he worked in an Irish pub in

Kilburn before getting a 'proper' job with Honeywell Computers as a programmer/operator.

"We were working with cards and paper tape rolls that had the holes punched into them. I'd done a course in computing as part of my degree but this was the late 1960s and although The University of London had one computer, it wasn't at Queen Mary!"

Around the same time, the Irish Government had made the bold decision to buy a couple of computers and word went round Honeywell that they were looking for a couple of 'lads' to go to Dublin and work the nightshift.

John Fisher volunteered, going to Dublin for four weeks at a time and working night shifts five nights a week.

Back in London, a friend mentioned that programmers were wanted in Iran.

"I attended an interview in a suite in the Savoy Hotel. They were looking to appoint a 'systems analyst' but didn't seem bothered that I was only a programmer."

John Fisher spent 18 months in Tehran working on an army payroll project.

"I'd spend every weekend exploring, walking up in the mountains and so on. One weekend, my roommate Joe and I took the bus into the centre of the city to the bazaar. It was only months later that Joe admitted how terrified he'd been. The bazaar had been completely packed with people and we didn't know our way around nor could we speak the language!"

It was around this time that John Fisher became more environmentally aware and when his contract ended, he persuaded his employers to let him exchange his air ticket for a rail one.

"I more or less dropped out when I came back from Iran. I bought a house in Dublin and shared it with people who were very into macrobiotics. I used to make bread, having ground the wheat myself, and sell it to wholefood shops. The trouble is, when you start applying principles, it can be very hard to find work!"

John Fisher found himself back in Suffolk in 1984, living in Ipswich then later Diss, while working as a cab driver. He went on to work in Youth Hostels in Colchester and Blaxhall, then returned to Saxmundham and later trained to be a driving instructor.

Among many voluntary activities, John Fisher is currently Chair of Saxmundham Town Council, a founding Governor of Saxmundham Free School and a member of Suffolk Libraries Board.

Melvin Freeman b.1962

"I've had some falls, I really have, but I've always ended up fine. I think I must be lucky, like a cat with nine lives!"

Melvin Freeman has been cleaning windows since he was eight years old and his mother suggested he borrow a ladder and try to earn some pocket money. He was born and brought up in Church Lodge, Saxmundham, one of six children; two step brothers, two step sisters and one brother.

"I was quite naughty in those days, all the time we were playing air rifles and climbing trees. The field behind Manor Gardens used to be the football field and we were up there a lot. I fell out of the window at home once. I couldn't be bothered to go downstairs and down the garden to have a pee so I balanced on a sill. I fell out, just missed the concrete slab, but I was fine, I got up, very lucky really."

After leaving school, Melvin Freeman worked at various jobs including on a farm carting grain and at Sizewell A, always doing windows in his spare time.

In his mid-thirties after his second marriage had ended in divorce, Melvin Freeman found himself homeless.

"There's nothing worse than having nowhere to live. Really. It's terrible. I was lucky that someone I knew said that I could stay in one of his caravans down in Kelsale. I was there until the doctor wrote to the council telling them that they had to find me a house on account of my bad asthma. I needed somewhere clean and dry to live."

He moved to Leiston, where he still lives, commuting to Saxmundham by bus or bicycle.

"I keep busy with all sorts of work; painting and decorating, gardening and so on. I had a bad fall last winter and it put me out for three months but I'm up and about again now. It won't be long before I've been working at windows for 50 years – I think I'll retire from it then!"

Maureen Godfrey b.1938

"One of the best things about growing up in Saxmundham was going to the dances in the Market Hall on a Saturday night. I used to go with my friend Ann and there was live music for jive and ballroom. The dances were run by a chap called Alfie Clarke and then they were taken over by Dennis Page and Kay Goddard."

Maureen Godfrey and her friend Ann were also both lucky recipients of invitations to join the audience for 'Wilfred Pickles in Have a Go' which visited the 'Urban District of Saxmundham' in December 1957. The 175 members of the audience at the Market Hall had been drawn from hundreds of applications to the Council Offices. The hugely popular radio show gave six contestants the chance to win financial prizes for 'sharing their secrets'. It was said to have over 20 million listeners.

Maureen Godfrey, nee Everett, grew up on Fairfield Road. After attending the County Primary on Fairfield Road, she started work at 15 at Judy Holland Hairdressers on Chantry Road.

"I was working on reception and the Wages Inspector came in. I told him what I was being paid, which wasn't enough, and Judy Holland sacked me!

After that, I went to work at Ray Gardiner's shoe shop on the corner of the Market Place. When Mr Gardiner closed that shop, I went on the train to work at a shop in Halesworth."

Saxmundham Picture House was at the bottom of Church Hill, on the site now occupied by Tesco.

"We used to go to the cinema and sit in the shillings. All the courting couples used to sit down the sides in the 'cuddle seats'!"

Maureen Godfrey met her husband while she was working in Halesworth and set up home with him in Leiston where they had two daughters, Teresa and Suzanne, and continue to live.

Raymond Green b.1942

Raymond Green was three and his mother pregnant with his sister, Marian, when his father was killed on D-Day.

"After Dad died, we came to stay with Mum's sister, Mrs Bowland, on Fairfield Road. It turned out to be a nice place for a boy to grow up, my Auntie on one side and Auntie's husband's family on the other."

Raymond Green's mother married Fred Hadley, a divorcee who lived nearby with two sons of his own, Brian and Michael.

"When I left school, I worked for a little while for Harry Lyon who had a funeral business on Chapel Road. Then in 1958, I joined the railway and worked there until I retired in 1985."

The trains that came through Saxmundham were powered by steam and the station itself had a continuous platform with a small gate so that passengers could be let through.

"I remember we all watched when Princess Margaret came up on the train to stay at Sternfield House. She travelled in an ordinary train, in first class. There were some lovely steam trains in those days; Britannia Class and Sandringham Class."

There were plenty of jobs to keep junior railway staff busy.

"I had to look after the signal lamps. I had to carry the paraffin and the wicks, walking along the tracks to the home signals and distant signals at Benhall, Brick Kiln and at the junction. They all had to be re-lit every seven days, your feet got quite tired.

"After that, I went up the junction box and looked after the first trains going to Sizewell on the track that had originally been used to carry stones to Garratt's in Leiston. If it hadn't been for Sizewell, Beeching would have closed that line."

Saxmundham junction was the point at which the line diverged; one heading north to Darsham, the other east towards Aldeburgh. The first stop on the Aldeburgh line was at Leiston where a siding had been built to carry materials and goods to and from Richard

Garratt's 'Works'. The eastward line went on to the marshes at Sizewell, a facility that had originally been built to transport cattle but which became essential in the construction of the nearby nuclear power stations, before continuing through Thorpeness and terminating at Aldeburgh.

"It was a bit cold working up the junction in the winter but the views of the countryside and the wildlife were beautiful. We had paraffin lamps and a coal stove to make a cup of tea. I used to walk to Bank Cottages, near Street Farm Road in Sax, to collect water for our kettle."

Saxmundham junction box was demolished in 1972 and the buildings at Aldeburgh station demolished and the land built upon in 1975. The line to Sizewell is still in use.

"In my last years with the railway, I stood in when the crossing keepers had a day off. Mostly at Willow Marsh at Darsham and Blackstock at Wickham Market.

I stayed in Sax at the end of the 1980s to care for Auntie and then Mum got Alzheimers and had to go into a home. My sister and I thought that a big four bedroom house was too big for me by myself, and at the same time, a place here in Henley Close became free. There's a nice social club here with lunches and keep fit and games nights. I also work as a steward at Saxmundham Museum."

John Hayward b.1942

Hayward's Plumbers and Building Supplies was a feature of Saxmundham High Street for more than 200 years. A glass window over the door of number four says 'Harry Hayward Plumber Est. 1770'. John Hayward is Harry Hayward's great, great, grandson.

Hayward's premises once took up the entire High Street-Church Road corner, encompassing what is now Emma K Framing and the houses beyond, now called Hayward's Mews.

Until the early 20th century, the business was run from a private house and the trades of painting and plumbing were managed in the yard behind.

By the 1950s, Hayward's employed 50 people, including bricklayers and labourers, carpenters, joiners, painters, decorators, plumbers and heating engineers. There were also staff in the retail shop, yard and office.

As a child, John Hayward remembers walking to the memorial field with his father, a Royal Observer Corps member, to see the doodlebugs overhead.

After Saxmundham Primary School Infants, he became a boarder at Brandeston Hall and Framlingham College, which meant that he didn't get to know many local children.

"I spent my holidays out of doors, playing in the bomb craters on the levels or biking round looking for the bench marks for the OS maps. I went bird nesting, something no one would do now, and spent many hours playing on the woodpiles in Father's wood yard."

Eventually, in 1990, the Hayward's closed, the site was redeveloped and new shops and residential properties built. John Hayward, who had taken over the business from his father in 1974, moved to Lancashire where he worked as a Building Maintenance Manager at Bolton Institute.

"In 1995 many people over 50 were offered early retirement, and since my partner at the time, family and friends were in Suffolk, I accepted and came back."

Today, John Hayward lives in Leiston with his partner, Christine, and invests considerable time and energy into his passion, beekeeping;

"My Grandfather kept bees and I have a photo of his hives. I remember as a young boy looking into a hive, I just remember the parallel bars, which I now know as tops of frames, I couldn't believe there were bees in there. I started keeping bees myself around 1980. When the business closed and I moved to Lancashire, I became treasurer of Manchester Beekeepers."

John Hayward has a daughter from his first marriage to Susan Martin: a farmer's daughter from Blythburgh.

John Jackson b.1932

John Jackson's story is so entwined in Saxmundham, it can be hard to know where to start. Albion Street, where he was born and lives now (albeit in different houses) is the obvious place.

"I was born at what is now number 27, although in those days, the houses didn't have numbers. My father was step-brother to the Martin Brothers who had the outfitters on the High Street [the premises most recently occupied by the Cotton Tree].

My great uncle was a prominent Salvation Army man called Tom Jackson. He had a sister who became pregnant with my father and later married a man called Bob Martin – so my father was a Jackson not a Martin.

In WW1, my father, James, worked on the railway on the Bury line, along which they sent the munitions to Harwich and Dover. He and his work-mates lived in huts beside the railway line and worked all the hours of daylight. When he had a day off, he went into Bury, which is where he met my mother.

My mother and her sisters had been in service in London, but when war broke out, the gentry had shut up their London houses and dismissed their staff. My mother got a job at The Angel Hotel.

They were married in 1918 and came to live in Albion Street in what was known as 'the yard', six houses that shared one tap at the back. My Grandmother lived next-door-but-one with her husband, Bob Martin, and their two sons."

The Martin brothers began their business careers making jams and pickles and gradually raised enough funds to buy a shop in Saxmundham Market Place that is now the newsagent, coincidentally currently called 'Martins'. Success in that premises enabled them to open 'Martin Bros' on the High Street.

"When WW2 broke out, Uncle Alec and Uncle Jack decided that one of them should stay and look after the business interests which were the shop and The Angel pub. Because he was the driving force, Alec stayed behind and joined the Home Guard whereas Jack joined the RAF. My father had been running The Angel and when Jack moved my grandparents into the pub, my mother and father came to Albion Street where my brother Edward and I were born."

Eventually, John Jackson's Uncle Alec sold the business and his father retired.

Having left Saxmundham Primary School at 14, John Jackson started work at Wightman's Garage on Bigsby's corner.

"To be honest, the War years in Sax had been the most exciting time of my life, what with the doodlebugs and all the soldiers about. Working in a garage seemed very dull, so when I was 17 and a half, I joined the Army."

John Jackson spent five years in REME. After basic and trade-specific training on armoured vehicles, he was posted to Japan and then on to Korea.

"When I came out of the army, I went back to the garage but found it very boring so I left there and started driving for Belle Coaches. At around that time, one of my friends set me up on a blind date with Mary Trelease and we just clicked. We were married in 1959 and moved to what used to be 3 Albion Street and is now number 5."

At around that time, John Jackson left Belle Coaches to work with the cattle at Street Farm before going to work at Sizewell A. The Jacksons had eight children, including two adoptees: Stephanie, Gilbert, Martin, Francis, Angela, John, Denise and Stewart. Needing more space, the couple took a council house on Park Avenue before moving to Saxon Road and then back to Albion Street.

"We'd made bread for years for ourselves. And then we ended up making rolls for the Scouts and the Guides, when I was Skipper and Mary was Akela. Then we got involved fundraising for the High School and made rolls for that.

When the bread strike came along in 1978, I was away at Scout camp. When I came back, Mary had given away all the bread that we had in the freezer and we had neighbours knocking at the door for more. I'd taken time off to do some decorating after I came back from camp but spent the whole time making bread. I was even making rolls for the canteen at Sizewell!

After my leave was over, I said to my boss that I didn't have time to come to work. He said, 'if you work as hard for yourself as you do for me, you'll do!' I arranged to take my superannuation and that was how the business started. Mary agreed that I'd better do it because otherwise I'd get to 65 and regret never having given it a go."

After continuing to bake from home for around a year (when he requested a Public Health inspection because he was selling food from home, the inspector replied, 'well someone's got to do it') John Jackson's bank manager told him that part of 'Hubbard's old place' [between the station and the car park] had become available and that he ought to rent it.

"I bought a broken mixer from Smiths in Aldeburgh and repaired it and found an oven on a scrap heap at Beccles and repaired that too."

A second bread strike brought a greater ever demand to the business and when the premises owner decided to sell, a small inheritance left to Mary Jackson enabled them to buy the bakery.

"A competitor in Halesworth went under so we took over some of his customers and eventually bought the remaining half of the bakery premises. We got more and more business, with three delivery rounds; Ipswich, Halesworth and the local one. We were supplying virtually all the local sub Post Offices in the days when there were village shops with Post Offices attached."

Initially, Jackson's sold to customers from the bakery premises but, because it wasn't visible to passing trade, John Jackson decided to buy the shop in the Market Place, which opened about a decade after the business started. At that point, Jackson's had two shops in Ipswich, one in Halesworth, plus the one in Saxmundham.

When independent bakeries began to be pushed out by supermarkets, Jackson's rented their premises to other businesses, from sandwich shops to a tattoo parlour and a Salvation Army charity shop.

"I haven't really retired, I'm the office boy! I gave up the hard work in the '90s when I had an internal haemorrhage and ended up in the Norfolk and Norwich. I won't retire until I die, Mary's the same, as long as I take money out of the business, I want to work for it!"

Patricia Langford b.1951

Pat Langford's great grandfather had a butchers shop in Saxmundham
High Street: Dalby Butcher and Poulterer.

"My great grandfather was Joe Dalby and his son was Arthur and
his son, my uncle Douglas, all ran the butcher's shop. Arthur Dalby
was apparently quite a character with various business interests,
including the butcher's shop in Saxmundham and one in Aldeburgh."

Joe Dalby built two houses on Chantry Road, handsome bay-
windowed properties set back and from the road and joined to each
other by an archway, now occupied by a garage.

"There was a slaughterhouse at the back of the houses, through
the archway, and the cattle would be driven up there from the sale
yard in Saxmundham or from further afield such as Halesworth."

Pat Langford was born in Chantry Road and when she was old
enough, went to Saxmundham Primary School in Fairfield Road
and then on to Saxmundham Modern School. She has one older
sister, Dorothy. Her father died when she was just 11.

"I was very happy at the Primary School when Jack Revell
was the Headmaster. I left Sax Modern at 15 but I didn't want to
because I loved history so much!"

After school, she worked in Clarke's grocers and café on the
High Street, staying there for 15 years, until the owner, Claude
Clarke died.

"After I left Clarke's, I went to work at RAF Bentwaters in the
canteen. I just loved it. It was so nice getting the chance to meet
people from all those other cultures, I remember talking to someone
from Thailand about the Thai style of cooking eggs!"

When RAF Bentwaters closed in 1993, Pat Langford worked at
Newton Commercial on the Eastlands Industrial Estate in Leiston,
a small factory that makes interior trim for classic cars.

"My work there went to three days a week and at that point,
I came back to Saxmundham and took a job at Chantry House

because it meant that I could be closer to my Mum, who was getting elderly."

Pat Langford's mother died in 2002.

"I've been working at Hollesley Bay prison in operations support for 12 years now, which means that I help administer the mail, process visitors and issue prisoners with work licences. It's an open prison and there are just over 400 prisoners. The staff are really nice, there's a real sense of camaraderie."

Penny Ling b.1964

Penny Ling was eleven when she first landed in Suffolk. Her father, an American serviceman, had been posted to Bentwaters near Rendlesham and she, her British mother, sister and three brothers settled happily on the base there.

"My Mom knew about the importance of integration and worked at the Anglo-American youth club in Saxmundham."

Sadly, Penny Ling lost her mother when she was just 15.

A week after her 16th birthday, she married funeral director Tony Brown's eldest son, Stephen, and set up home in the houses adjacent to the ambulance station in Saxmundham. The couple had two daughters, Laura and Angie, and Penny Ling worked in the town's youth club.

When the marriage ended she moved to what's known locally as 'the American Estate', houses built for US service families stationed in Suffolk during the Cold War on roads named 'Mayflower' and 'Lincoln', (although it was by then in British ownership). Penny Ling had another daughter, Bethany. It was whilst living on the estate that she met her second husband, David Ling, a 'Saxmundham boy'.

Penny Ling spent three years working for CYDS, a dedicated support service for disadvantaged young people based in Leiston and Saxmundham.

"One of my proudest moments was when Saxmundham Town Council had one ticket for someone to go and see the Queen when she came to Ipswich and I was awarded that ticket!"

Penny Ling had to leave CYDS when her husband became ill and she needed to be at home to take care of him. She now works in the newsagent in the Market Place.

"There's something about Saxmundham – I've tried to leave it twice and once even sold my house intending to return to the US and couldn't go through with it! On another occasion, I was going to move to Bury but I couldn't do it!

Saxmundham is a town that looks after itself, I've never known a town like it. I'm really proud of our town and of places like the Museum. I do what I can to help."

Francis 'Mac' McBurney b.1945

Mac McBurney was born above the fish and chip shop in Aldeburgh where his mother worked. His father was in the Merchant Navy. When he was eight, the family moved to Yoxford.

"We used to come to Sax all the time; to the pictures, on sale days and nearly always on Saturdays. Usually, we'd walk to Darsham and get the train to Sax from there. We'd spend an hour in Clarke's having a cup of tea and then we'd go along to Hubbards and sit cross-legged on the floor watching the TV – it nearly always seemed to be the Lone Ranger! Geoff Hubbard was really good, he didn't mind us being there at all. Then we'd go to the Picture House."

When he was 12, Mac McBurney left Yoxford Primary School and was one of the first intake of children at the Modern School in Saxmundham.

"It was wonderful but a bit scary because it was so big. I cycled every day from Yoxford because we lived the wrong end of the town for me to qualify for the school bus!

I stayed at the Modern until I was 16 – you were able to leave at 15 – because I wanted to take the qualifications to join the Merchant Navy." Mac McBurney joined P&O Cruises and, by the time he was 21, had been on six world cruises.

"I don't think I appreciated how lucky I was. This was the early 1960s and the passengers were very well-to-do; lots of Lords and Ladies and very wealthy people. Then there were the £10 people. There was a scheme in those days that allowed you to emigrate to Australia for £10 as long as you had a job. Mind you, the £10 people lived below decks! Things were very different in those days."

After 10 years working on cruise ships, Mac McBurney took a break and a number of jobs in Saxmundham, including as a delivery driver for grocers Hartley & Algar on the High Street.

"There were three main grocers in Sax in those days; the International Stores, the Co-op, and Hartley & Algar, which was the up-market one. I made deliveries on a trade bike all around the local area and eventually graduated to a van! It was good fun and very interesting. I also worked for Geoff Hubbard's audio electrical business for a little while, it was a company he ran from the back of the shop.

"Of course sale days on a Wednesday were the time to be in Sax. Like everyone, we used to go the The Angel, but we also used to buy a chicken from the sale and play pokey die for it at the back of the Queens! Ted Ballard was the landlord then.

"Saturday nights were dance nights at the Market Hall – everyone used to go. I used to carry the drums in for the drummer which meant that I got in for free!"

Mac McBurney married Beryl (nee Clouting) in 1971 and they went on to have two sons, Alex and Stuart. The family moved to Park Avenue in Saxmundham in 1974 which is where they still live.

"I went back on to the boats for about 10 years in the early '70s, but this time only the roll-on, roll-off ferries from Felixstowe to Antwerp and Harwich to the Hook of Holland.

When I eventually came off the boats in 1977, I went to work for Relums which was an import-export business on the industrial estate in Sax.

After a couple of years, I went to work as a driver for Hatcher Components and I was there until I retired. I loved working as a lorry driver, meeting people, seeing different places.

"I love Saxmundham. When we moved here, you'd get up on Sunday morning and find a bag of potatoes or carrots or something hanging on your door. Everyone grew veg in those days and people were very kind."

Sandra Moore b.1941

Sandra Moore was born in Saxmundham and spent her early years in the town, attending Saxmundham Primary before going on to Leiston Grammar School. She moved away to go to University in Durham before moving back to Saxmundham thirty years later when her grandchildren were born.

During her working years, she came to Saxmundham most weekends to visit family.

"I was born in Church House on Church Hill, where my grandfather had his blacksmith's forge. Some of my earliest memories are of the smell of hot iron cooling on horses' hooves and the sizzle of hot metal in the cooling tank.

I also remember hiding under a Morrison shelter, which was like a heavy steel-topped table with a mesh cage underneath that we had in the kitchen at Church House.

Walking beside the sale meadow, you would see ponies tied up, even in the 1950s. Even though there were plenty of cars about by then, it was not unusual for the older country boys, including my grandfather, to continue using a pony and trap."

When she was six, Sandra Moore moved to the farm at the top of Church Hill, now known as Wood Farm, which was then owned by Squire Long. Her father and his two brothers ran the farm with part-time workers as needed, for harvest, for example. There was a Suffolk Punch called Boxer who pulled the wagons.

"Many of my strongest childhood memories involve places where particular trees and flowers grew and of the miles of hedges now no longer in existence.

There were several woods on the farm, the ones near the Leiston road are all gone, except for the strip dividing the farm driveway from Manor Gardens.

Manor Gardens was then a field containing a stackyard [A farmyard or enclosure where stacks of hay or straw in sheaf are stored]. We were always being warned to 'watch the hay knife!'. "

The 'Big Wood' was to the right of the Saxmundham to Leiston Road, about half way between the farm lane and the house called Wardspring.

"I always enjoyed finding my hornbeam there, with its pagoda-like catkins, as it seemed to be the only one around. We knew where the nut trees grew and where to find the wild strawberries on the verge beside the wood. On the far side of the wood, there was a clay bottomed pond with such clear water that you could stand for ages watching the water life."

After university, Sandra Moore worked in Essex and Norfolk in the Youth Employment Service, as a teacher in Leiston, and finally as a civil servant in London.

Her daughter, Belinda, is the author of this book.

Christopher Newson b.1951

"I first met Maggi Hambling in 2007. I'd been playing the part of King Arthur in Cinderella at The Theatre Royal in Norwich and, with the money I'd earnt, I'd bought a camera and video equipment.

"I'd always loved her Scallop at Aldeburgh and managed to take a picture of it with a rainbow reaching out of the top. It took loads of phone calls to arrange to meet her, but when I did, she really loved the image and used it on her calling card."

Chris Newson went on to make a film of the Scallop for Maggi Hambling called 'Storm', set to Benjamin Britten's piece 'Storm' from his opera Peter Grimes.

"She'd come over to my studio for a production meeting about the video and had seen a picture that I'd painted with acrylic. She asked who'd done it and when I told her it was me, she told me to paint another and then another and then another. The one after that I sold for £200."

Christopher Newson began painting in prison, where he was serving a three year sentence for the supply of Class A drugs. "I started an art class to relieve the boredom."

He was released after 24 months and returned to Saxmundham, where his first son was born.

"I was with him until he was 3, but then my addictions took hold and he ended up being brought up by his mum in Milton Keynes. He's 25 now, and I'm blessed that we're in touch again."

Christopher Newson was born in Blenheim Terrace on Saxmundham High Street. He was the eldest of three.

"I was only three when we moved to my grandmother's house in Park End. My Mum left when I was four and, when I was six, my Dad died, so my grandparents, Mr and Mrs Edmunds, bought us up. Tim and Sally were so young, they don't really remember our Dad, but I do."

Christopher Newson left school at 15 to begin a welding

apprenticeship. This was followed by a electrical apprenticeship and finally a job at Sizewell A in the Health Physics Department, which lasted six months.

"I went travelling and ended up working in Amsterdam. When I came home, I got a job as a cocktail waiter at Bentwater's Air Base and that was the point when I was prosecuted for selling drugs and ended up in prison."

The first of four periods of rehab followed.

"I'd been at a rehab centre in Norwich and had become friends with an actor called Peter Moynihan, who'd appeared in the early Oxo commercials. When we got out, he took me to see the Maddermarket Theatre in Norwich where I became a volunteer stage carpenter and caught the acting bug.

"I went on to study performing arts at college in Wisbech for two years and qualified with a distinction. I then went on to a masters at the Royal Welsh College of Music and Drama. I lasted 18 months of a three year course."

After a second period of rehab, Christopher Newson applied to complete his degree at Ipswich School of Performing Arts where he achieved a 2.1. He went on to begin a PGCE but relapsed six months into the course.

It was after the following period of rehab that he won the role of King Arthur in Norwich.

"By 2009, I had been sober for three years and my son Timmy was born. I lived very happily with him and his mum in Saxmundham.

"Things began to go wrong in 2010 when I was diagnosed with Hepatitis C and prescribed a year's chemotherapy. I got to hear the prognosis the day after my younger brother Tim's funeral – he had died of cancer.

"My treatment, and everything else that was going on, put a lot of stress on the relationship between me and Timmy's mum. I relapsed and ended up in a clinic in Lowestoft. It was here that I learnt about AA [Alcoholics Anonymous] which has been a big part of my life ever since.

"I'm very lucky to have Maggi Hambling as my mentor. She sponsors me with oil paint every month and understands my struggles with addiction.

"I'm glad I'm back in Sax. I feel safe here – I know everyone and everyone knows me. I can't imagine being anywhere else."

Denis Nichols b.1928
Derek Nichols b.1953

Denis Nichols grew up in the idyllic surroundings of Parham Hall where his father was Head Gardener. He played in the meadows, watched his father's beehives and attended Wickham Market School, where he learnt to play the piano and organ, a skill he continues to use today.

In 1942, he joined Ashfords in Saxmundham on a three year apprenticeship as a cabinet maker.

"Ashfords was the big department store in Saxmundham High Street, where Flicks is now. They sold furniture and home furnishings and also made coffins."

In 1946, Denis Nichols began three years of Military Service with the RAF, working on the wooden air frames of Mosquito fighter-bombers.

"The Flying Fortresses were just next door to where we lived at Parham, you could almost feel the air move when they went overhead."

After returning from Military Service, he came back to Ashfords and continued to work in the firm's furniture manufacture and repair department.

"I married Hilda in 1950 and we had four children; Derek, Mary, Eileen and David. We lived in Reydon at first – I was working at Ashfords – and I played the organ at Wangford, deputising at Southwold. We were only about a year in Reydon because I became ill and we moved back to Parham to stay with Mum and Dad.

My Dad kept 28 beehives – we never went without sugar in the war."

By the time Derek Nichols came along in 1953, the family had moved to the Red House on South Entrance which was customarily the Ashfords's manager's house. They went from there to the newly-built houses on Saxon Road before moving on to Fairfield Road.

Denis Nichols remained at Ashfords making furniture repairs and coffins.

"We used to come up to Herlocks, the saw mills in St John's Road, and get a whole tree at a time."

Whilst at Ashfords, Denis Nichols qualified as a Funeral Director. In the 1970s, he branched out on his own, working as an independent Funeral Director from home.

"It's a full time job because you're on call night and day. I had the business for ten years – Tony Brown started out with me – and then East of England Co-op came along and bought the business.

I stayed working for the Co-op until I retired. They got a good deal because as well as being a funeral director, I would play the organ!

Since I retired, I still play the organ most Sundays, mostly at Yoxford. Of course I miss the old days, you knew everyone here then."

Derek Nichols grew up in Saxmundham and says that he got his love of plants and horticulture from his grandfather.

After leaving school at 15, he became an apprentice at Notcutts Nurseries and in his spare time, began buying and selling plants, planting the seeds for the business that trades outside the Market Hall every Saturday.

"I was very busy with the Youth Club in my 20s. There was a mixture of English and American kids. I'd be up there nearly every night, we had parties and went to youth festivals – it was a marvellous time. I suppose I was involved in that for about ten years."

Having had experience of running discos at the Youth Club, Derek Nichols set up 'HiFi Sound'.

"We did weddings and parties, that sort of thing, until I was in my mid-30s. when I stopped HiFi Sound, I helped one of my friends run 'Stateside Disco' which we did until we'd turned 50 when it seemed enough was enough!"

Derek Nichols left Notcutts after 16 years, planning to set up his own business. Personal circumstances meant that he ended up working with his dad at the Co-op, growing and selling plants in his spare time.

"It was too much though, a lot of travelling, so I made the decision to do the plants full time."

Derek Nichols misses the Saxmundham of his youth; "You couldn't hardly walk along the pavement on a Saturday morning, it was heaving. Sale day on a Wednesday was even busier – we used to bunk off school to go down to that."

Left to right: Derek Nichols, Denis Nichols

Bryony Peall b.1976

Bryony Peall was born in Ipswich Hospital in 1976, second to arrive after her twin Nathan. She also has an older brother, William.

Her mother was leader of the WRVS playgroup in Saxmundham for 17 years and Bryony and her twin attended there and also spent time at Rendham Playgroup (to give their mum a break!).

She went to school at Saxmundham Primary School and then continued to Saxmundham Middle School before transferring to Thomas Mills High School in Framlingham.

"I hated Thomas Mills and missed my friends. Eventually, I got moved to Leiston High School where I sat my GCSEs and A Levels.

As a teen, I developed a ridiculous desire to escape Saxmundham as soon as humanly possible. The moment school was out, I worked as hard as I could to raise money for a round-the-world ticket and spending money."

Escape she did, just a few days after her 19th birthday, to travel extensively in Africa, Australia, India and Thailand. After two years, she found that she missed Saxmundham and returned to have her first child, Harriet, in 1997.

Bryony Peall embarked on a second adventure when her daughter was a toddler.

"We travelled through much of India and Venezuela. Because she was so small, Hattie opened my eyes to seeing the world in a different light."

They came home in time for her daughter to start at Saxmundham Primary School at which point, Bryony Peall enrolled on a Foundation Degree course at Suffolk College. She graduated in 2005 and became Manager of The Cut in Halesworth after which she became Personal Assistant to Liz Calder, founder of Bloomsbury Publishing and resident of Saxmundham.

Her second child, Finnian, was born in 2006.

Bryony Peall was elected to Saxmundham Town Council in 2007, and served four years before becoming frustrated by the red tape that appeared to be strangling local initiatives.

She has been a committed member of St John's Ambulance since childhood, being awarded 'Best Cadet in East Anglia' in her teens and then second best in the country when her brigade made it to the finals of the national championships. For the past eight years she has led the Badgers, 5 to 10 year-old St John's members.

"Over the years, my opinion of Saxmundham has undergone a complete transformation. Growing up, I thought it was full of dull farmer types with no aspirations. My time away has made me crave it and despite many opportunities to leave, I keep being drawn back.

Sax has more than doubled in my lifetime and is full of amazing, inspirational people who have become friends. I still like to go off exploring but like best being able to come back home!"

Peter Pemberton b.1945

"It was like growing up in the Garden of Eden," says Peter Pemberton of his childhood in Phalerom, on the Greek coast south of Athens, "I had two brothers and a sister, the sea was clean and the beach was beautiful."

His English father had been in Burma during the War, a member of the Chindits, a British special forces unit whose mission was to disrupt the building of the Burma railway by the Japanese. Peter Pemberton's mother was Greek, born in Alexandria.

"After the War, my father worked for the Commonwealth War Graves Commission, establishing a cemetery at Phalerom."

Peter Pemberton completed his education at boarding school in England after which he moved to Montreal in Canada where he worked for five years in heavy industrial engineering.

"I'd come back to Europe and was staying with Mum and Dad in Gallipoli; Dad was still with the War Graves Commission. One morning, Mum saw an advertisement for a 'Holiday Guide' in Greece and suggested I apply for it.

I was sent a telegram to go to London for an interview and then I flew to Athens, starting as a rep for Clarkson's Holidays, at the time, the biggest holiday company in the country."

By 1972, Peter Pemberton was in Crete, working with Clarkson's Holidays in Malia, then a quiet village bordered by sandy beaches. When the company went bust, he stayed on, opening his own bar, 'Malia by Night', and then Malia's first disco, 'Sundown'.

"In 1975, I came to visit my sister for Christmas. I went to The Bell and it was full of local characters, a rich tapestry, very funny. I loved the Suffolk countryside and the people."

It was around this time that Peter Pemberton became 'Pete the Greek', an epithet by which he's known still.

Famous stories abound, including one featuring Peter O'Toole who had apparently come to stay at The Bell (chosen because it was close to a station with a direct line to London) to learn some lines.

"There was this guy at the bar and he looked like Peter O'Toole, so we kept calling him Peter. He was very good company but modest, didn't talk about himself at all. We took him to Aldeburgh one night and ended up playing dice in the Cross Keys. Very funny nights, it was only when he left that the receptionist confirmed that it really was O'Toole."

"I met a lovely young lady from Aldeburgh and we had a nice romance but I had to go back to Crete. When I returned to Saxmundham, we settled down together and had two children, both now in their 20s."

Today, Peter Pemberton is best known for his restaurant businesses, including Zorba's on Saxmundham Marketplace.

"My first business was an off licence called 'Leiston Wines and Spirits' on Leiston High Street; I then opened a second one in Woodbridge and then a restaurant in Woodbridge called 'El Greco'. Once I'd sold this in 1988, I opened a launderette in Leiston and then a kebab shop in Leiston, then a kebab shop in Fram and in 2002 Zorba's in Saxmundham followed by Rossini's in Fram in 2003!

I like to keep busy, I like people, I don't like spending my time in front of the TV."

A significant part of Peter Pemberton's life now involves taking care of his father, now widowed and in his late 90s, living in Leiston.

"I keep a place on Limnos and would like to spend more time in Greece. We have holidays there but I won't go back because of Dad."

Albert Pond b.1923

Albert Pond was not yet 20 when the convoy carrying the 7th Armoured Division was ambushed on its way to Port Suez, "two ships went down, one carrying nurses to work in the field hospital. We'd been told to take 'boat stations' which meant that we were lined up on deck. We saw them drown. It was terrible."

Albert Pond spent his early years in Huntingdon, one of seven children. His father had a successful charabanc (motor coach) company. As for so many families, life changed drastically as a result of the General Strike. The charabanc business was taken over by Eastern Counties Omnibus Company and the family was moved to Ipswich. "There was one charabanc that had been converted to a rescue vehicle. Father loaded everything up and off we went, Mother, Father and seven children squeezed into the cab."

Albert Pond's father used the proceeds of the business to buy a piece of land onto which he built a house and a smallholding with pigs and chickens.

"One of the things that Father did manage to arrange was for his sons to have apprenticeships at Eastern Counties. When I was 14, I left school and went to the depot for a three and a half year apprenticeship working on Gardner Diesel Engines."

Shortly before his 18th birthday, Albert Pond went to the forces recruitment office in Norwich Road, Ipswich, hoping to join the RAF like his two older brothers.

"Stanley was in the Lancaster Squadron. They were up in Scotland practicing for the bouncing bombs. Tim was flying Hurricanes and was mentioned in dispatches for rescuing a Polish pilot by flying him back on his lap, with the plane's roof up. He landed them safely at Biggin Hill."

Albert Pond's experience on Gardner engines was, however, too much for the recruiting officers to overlook. Rather than the RAF, he was assigned to work on tanks whose engines were similar to the bus engines he knew so well.

"We had 12 months of severe training during which we quickly learnt that to be part of a tank crew of three, you needed to be made of cast iron. We thought it was hell on earth."

Albert Pond's tragically depleted convoy eventually docked in Port Suez, where the troops disembarked to a transit camp before being loaded onto cattle trucks the next morning for transportation to another transit camp the other side of Cairo.

"I'd never seen so many flies in all my life! As big as blow flies and they were out to nip you. We were only allowed two pints of water a day. You can imagine that in that heat, there wasn't enough drink, let alone to clean yourself properly. Men got ill and died from the flies."

Unimaginably harsh and inhospitable, the desert they landed in at El Alamein, around 60 miles from Alexandria, was a geographic bottleneck, the possession of which could prevent Nazi forces from sweeping up to the enemy position from the rear. It was generally considered to be the last stand for the Allies in Africa.

"Churchill had sent Montgomery to lead the 8th Army because the previous commander had been killed. Montgomery didn't look like he was up to the job at first but he grew into his role."

Severe training was insisted upon right up to 23rd October 1942, when 'all Hell would break loose'. Montgomery had grown in respect and position, telling troops before the battle began, 'I'm not Nelson, but I expect every man to do his duty. If we fail here, it's goodbye to England.'

Against all odds, Albert Pond survived three offensives in the desert.

"The Germans had superior tanks and weaponry. The only way was for us to get in between them. We all prayed."

The Desert Rats came home through Europe, "We were sent to

Austria to help relocate displaced persons. In 1945, I was with the Russians when they came to liberate Auschwitz."

In 1946, Albert Pond was stationed at Ufford Park near Woodbridge, a tank research station, "They were trying to get Valentine tanks to jump ditches by strapping rockets to the side. Unsuccessfully!"

It was while stationed in Ufford that he went out for the evening in Woodbridge with a fellow soldier and, when they thought they might be late getting back to barracks, 'borrowed' a couple of bikes from outside the fish and chip shop.

"The MPs and the civilian police called everyone out the next morning to find out who had taken the bikes - we'd put them in the guard room for safe-keeping! My friend and I owned up and I was

told to return the bike to the family of Colonel Fleming in Melton. It belonged to one of his wife's maids, a girl called Dorothy who I'd spotted in the fish and chip shop the previous evening.

Well, to cut a long story short, we were married in 1947 and stayed happily married until Dorothy sadly passed away last year."

Albert and Dorothy set up home in Dallinghoo and were soon joined by their son, David. Albert worked as a builder in Woodbridge for many years before retiring to Saxmundham.

Helen Revell b.1928

Helen Revell was born in Rhodesia (now Zimbabwe) where her father worked as a mining engineer. When the family returned to the UK in 1938, she went to school at Wycombe Abbey in Buckinghamshire, before it was requisitioned by the US military in 1942.

After completing school in St Andrews, she trained in domestic science at Gloucester College and came to Saxmundham in 1954 to set up home with her husband Jack.

"My husband found a job at Rendham Primary School and that enabled us to buy our first house. He cycled to Rendham every day from Saxmundham. In 1961 he moved from Rendham to Sax Primary."

Helen Revell taught domestic science at Leiston Grammar School and Leiston and Saxmundham Middle Schools. From 1961 to 1982, her husband was headmaster of Saxmundham Primary School.

"Jack had lost his hand during the War and was famous for shocking his pupils by suddenly pulling off his prosthetic hand while leading assemblies on the topic of safety!"

The couple had considered emigrating to Canada but Canadian immigration interviews were held in June and the UK school term didn't finish until July, so by the time they were able to attend, there were only areas like Arctic Canada remaining.

After retiring from teaching, Helen Revell became Town Recorder, an honorary position that she held until quite recently. She was a founding member of the Saxmundham History Society and a founder and trustee of Saxmundham Museum.

"Saxmundham seemed like a real metropolis when we moved here. We'd been living in a tiny village near Hadleigh that had just one shop. It was a happy place to live. We had Saxmundham Urban District Council, which meant that decisions were made locally and things were done quickly and appropriately by people who understood the town.

What makes me cross these days is the huge number of additional houses, with no supporting infrastructure or community facilities."

Helen Revell has three sons, five grandchildren and two great grandsons. Jack Revell was tragically killed in a road traffic accident on the A12 in 2004.

Sue Ryder Richardson b.1953

Sue Ryder Richardson's great grandfather, John Charles, bought
The Beeches (the beautiful Queen Anne house on North Entrance,
facing the end of Fairfield Road) along with the doctor's practice it
accommodated, in 1896.

"He'd been at Cambridge with Lord Cranbrook, who wrote to
him, saying, 'Ryder, I'm in need of a good doctor and there's a living
going in Saxmundham!'"

Dr John Charles Ryder Richardson took on the practice in
Saxmundham and so began a tradition that would last three
generations and nearly a century.

"My great grandfather had five children of whom my
grandfather, David, was the eldest. David also studied medicine at
Cambridge and worked in the practice alongside his father after
returning from naval service on HMS Devonshire in 1918.

John Charles died in 1929 and my grandfather then had the
sole practice until my father joined him in 1949. The surgery and
dispensary were in the Georgian part of the house with old Tudor
cottage kitchens behind. The living rooms were in the grander
Queen Anne part."

Dr David Ryder Richardson is still referred to as 'Dr David' by
many of Saxmundham's older residents. He relished the job of being
the doctor in a busy market town and didn't retire until he was 84.

"My grandfather was a remarkable character. He shone
academically but he also had a great sense of mischief. As a young
medic in London in 1915 he threw a snowball at a glamorous
young woman in Hyde Park. Using some French expletive she was
astounded to find the culprit responding in the same language.

This was the start of a long courtship between Marthe Paquet
and Dr David that lasted throughout the First World War. Despite
her having to return to France they continued their relationship
by letter. My grandfather even proposed by letter and sent a

magnificent diamond engagement ring through the regular post, rather amazingly it arrived safely and I have it today. Marthe was finally able to return to England in 1919, when they married.

My grandmother had moved into The Beeches before they were married and from letters she wrote to my grandfather, who seemed to have been based in London briefly, she obviously struggled living with future in-laws. In all the years that she was here, she never fully mastered the English Language and only ever used the present tense!"

Dr David and Marthe Ryder Richardson had three children, John, David and Helen. The boys went to school at Eversley in Southwold and then St Pauls in London. Helen was home educated until she was 14 and then went to St Felix.

"My Dad and uncle used to 'work their passage' on the train to London. They somehow managed to persuade the steward to let them work as waiters in the dining car so that they could travel for free. The money they saved they used to go to Harrods on a Saturday afternoon where they would buy a Camembert, this they kept in their lockers until it was ripe and ready to eat. They would then do the same the following week! It is not reported how many friends they had at school!

When he was about 6 or 7, my Dad was briefly friends with Prince Philip. My great-grandmother, Mary Elizabeth (married to John Charles), had been a nurse at St Thomas's Hospital in London where she had trained with the lady who became Prince Philip's nursemaid. Prince Philip at that time lived in Paris and was largely brought up by his nursemaid.

When they visited England, usually to stay at Somerleyton Hall, they stayed at The Beeches en route to Lowestoft. Prince Philip and my Dad played on the lawns and fought robustly about who was more important, doctors or kings! Philip, being slightly older and larger, always won."

After school, John and David both became doctors and Helen a pharmacist.

During his National Service in South Africa, John Ryder Richardson met his future wife, Eleanor Mosse.

"Eleanor had decided to emigrate to South Africa with her friend Hazel after a shattering time nursing during the war. She had been born in India, the fifth generation of her family to be born there, and so had no real ties with Britain.

She met John on a blind date in Durban and they fell in love. Apartheid was beginning and with her Indian heritage she was hard to place in the new South African society. She remained in South Africa for a year after John returned to enter GP partnership with his father in Saxmundham and in 1950 came to Suffolk to marry and become a GP's wife.

After they were married, my Mum and Dad moved into a tiny flat over the surgery at The Beeches. They had four children in four and a half years! My two sisters and I were born in the flat but shortly after my brother was born we moved to a house called Westhill on Rendham Road."

Sue Ryder Richardson and her siblings went to Mrs Russell's school in Fairfield Road, "It was known to everyone as Aunty Barbara's!" then to Fairfield Preparatory School in North Entrance and in the girls' case, to St Felix in Southwold. "My brother went on to Haileybury and then did his sixth form at Woodbridge School.

I studied English at York University and then got a very junior job in publishing. In 1977, I was offered the opportunity to help out at a fashion forecasting publishing house and eventually ended up taking over the UK side of their business when everyone moved to the States. The work and company have evolved over the years, but essentially I have been in Fashion Forecasting and PR since then and for the past 32 years have had the joys of commuting to London."

Sue Ryder Richardson married Bobby Rusack in 1981. They live in Sweffling, where they raised their now grown-up daughters, Katherine, Alexandra and Joanna.

"I remember growing up in Saxmundham so well. Mr Cousins used to drive the dustcart pulled by a white horse called Daisy. On Sundays we used to hang a duster out of the kitchen window and a boy would come along while we were at church and put a block of ice cream in the icebox and take the money off the kitchen table. It seems incredible now."

As a student, Sue Ryder Richardson worked behind the bar at The Bell Hotel.

"There were so many characters in those days. Charles Bravery, an artist arrived here to create sets for Benjamin Britten, and there was a chap called Tansy who used to bike in from Benhall. He would carefully turn his bike round to face Benhall before he came in to drink. One night, one of the local rascals turned his bike around and Tansy came back half an hour after leaving to announce that he'd 'got all a-way to Kelsale' before he realised he was going the wrong direction!"

Sue Ryder Richardson with her father Dr John

Dorothy Thompson b.1927

When Dorothy Thompson and her husband Ron moved to their new house on Saxon Road in 1950, she described as seeming 'like a palace' compared to the farmworkers' cottages in which she'd grown up.

"They built the houses on Saxon Road in blocks of eight, starting at the top. There was quite a waiting list because the houses were so spacious with two big living rooms, wide halls, proper bathrooms as well as downstairs toilets."

Dorothy Thompson was born in Knodishall and grew up in Little Glemham, attending Wickham Market Primary School. Her father was a horseman on nearby farms.

At 14, she entered service, starting as a scullery maid and going on to work at many large houses, including at White House Farm for Lord and Lady Cranbrook.

"The family were living at the Farm because the army were in Glemham Hall during the war."

She married Ron in 1947. Ron Thompson was born in Dennington in 1921 and moved to Albion Street as a small boy. His father worked at Bower's Coal Merchants which was where the car park at the back of the Market Place is now.

"Ron went to the Gas Works when he left school and he was a reserve fireman, just like his father. He joined the army when he was 18. He was posted to the Far East almost straight away to work on the railway but he was captured by the Japanese and interred as a Prisoner of War in Changi jail between 1942 and 1945.

We met when he came home. We had a land girl lodging with us at Benhall Low Street and she knew another POW. She asked if I'd go to the Picture House with them and then afterwards he asked if he could take us to The Angel for a drink. That's where I met Ron."

Their first son, Stephen, was born in 1948 and second son

Christopher in 1952. After being demobbed, Ron Thompson was sent on a course for ex-servicemen in Essex where he was taught to be a plasterer. He went on to work for Reades of Aldeburgh as a builder and plasterer, travelling between jobs on his motorbike.

In addition to her work as a mother and a wife, Dorothy Thompson had various jobs in and around Saxmundham including at the Queens Head (she and Ron had held their wedding reception in the upstairs ballroom) and as a Home Help.

"When I was in my late 20s, I took driving lessons with Mr Turner from Leiston. It was a great help because it made it much easier for me to get around and about to Friston and Kelsale and so

Ron and Dorothy Thompson (née Gilbert) at Benhall St Mary's Church in 1947

on for my Home Help work.

I really enjoyed it – people were so glad to see us. We did their meals, shopping, cleaning and so on and most importantly, we talked to them. They were very grateful, most were very lonely. There wasn't the terrible rush that there is today for carers."

When Swann House Nursing Home was built at the bottom of Saxon Road in 1999, Dorothy Thompson and many of her Home Help colleagues transferred there to work.

"We had our own group of people, many of whom were widows or widowers, and again, they really looked forward to seeing you."

Ron Thompson was a dedicated member of the Labour party and received a certificate for 50 years membership in 2008. He was also an expert gardener, with allotments as well as his home garden.

"He always kept a diary, like his father had done. I've got them all – there are notes of all sorts of things from the price of petrol, the time to plant out the spring cabbages, fire service call outs. I've also got a lovely letter that he received from King George VI, thanking him for his service. They're fascinating to have."

Dorothy Thompson is well known for the kindness and support she gives to friends and neighbours in and around Saxmundham. Her husband Ron now lives in a local care home. They have four grandchildren and four great-grandchildren.

Myrtle Turner b.1929

It's now 52 years since Myrtle Turner began leading Keep Fit classes in and around Saxmundham. She still runs four each week, three in the town, one in Great Glemham.

"In 1958, I was recovering from a period of illness and had lost a lot of confidence. I decided to take a Keep Fit class and loved it so much that I embarked on the training to become an instructor myself. I led my first class in 1962 and haven't looked back.

Someone asked me the other day if, because of my age and that of some of my class members, we did exercises sitting down? No way!" Myrtle Turner grew up in Sternfield. As teenagers, she and her friends used to bike into Saxmundham to go to the dances at the Market Hall.

"We'd have our dresses in little attaché cases on the back of our bikes and we would squeeze into what used to be tiny changing rooms to put our dresses and lipstick on. Those were the days!"

She married Clifford, known as Tim, in 1949 and the couple moved into one of the staff flats at Hurts Hall.

"It was lovely living at the Hall, just beautiful being surrounded by all the gardens and meadows."

Tim Turner worked at Saxmundham Urban District Council as a foreman, responsible for the upkeep of roads, pavements, drains and so on. Son Ivan was born in 1951 and it wasn't long before the family outgrew the Hurts Hall flat.

"There had been a rule about 'no children, no animals' in the flat, but when Ivan came along, they were so delighted to have a baby at the Hall after so many years, they didn't mind at all."

When Ivan was five, the family moved to Park Avenue in Saxmundham, a house with more bedrooms and family space.

"There was nothing modern about it at all. There was still the copper in the corner of the kitchen that you had to fill with buckets of water. When you wanted a bath, you had to pump the rotary pump that would send the water up to the bathroom. Hard work."

After 15 years in Park Avenue, the family moved to a small end-of-terrace cottage on Church Hill that had originally been a farm cottage belonging to Hurts Hall. After a few years, they bought the adjoining property and knocked through, creating the spacious house that Myrtle Turner still lives in today.

"This was a beautiful spot. There was farmland over the road and we had a large garden behind with fields beyond that. My husband had an allotment too and we grew all our own vegetables and he kept bees; at one point, we had 13 hives, some here, some boarded out, mostly on farms at Sternfield."

In addition to running Keep Fit classes and her home, Myrtle Turner worked in the Occupational Therapy Department at St Audry's Hospital in Melton for six years before going on to work at the Saxmundham Training Centre teaching life skills to adults with special needs.

"I miss all the wonderful shops we used to have in Saxmundham. Mr Clarke's grocers and café – they put on a roast dinner every day and nearly everyone who worked in the town went there for lunch.

On sale day, the farmers would bring their animals into the sale yard [now the Waitrose store and car park] to sell. While the men were busy buying and selling, the women would do the weekly shop and, after the sale, the men would meet in The White Hart to discuss the day's business. You knew everyone and everyone looked after each other."

As well as Keep Fit, Myrtle Turner has an hour-long early morning walk around Saxmundham every day of the week except weekends.

"It started when we had a dog and I used to go out to walk him. The dog died and I carried on!"

Joyce Vale b.1943

Joyce Vale was born in Stratford St Andrew, one of five children. Her family moved to Farnham when she was five. After leaving school, she worked in the canning factory in Woodbridge, a well-known local employer whose business was to preserve the many fruits and vegetables grown in East Suffolk.

"I worked in the fruit department mostly and it was a good job where you could make friends. They used to pick us up from Farnham in the Crane's bus and drop us in Woodbridge."

When she was 21, Joyce Vale (née Ling) married Frederick and they moved to Saxmundham to the houses at the back of the Market Place, along from where there was once a betting shop and in the location that is now home to Saxmundham Angling and Trophy Centre.

"I liked living in Sax, we used to go to the Picture House and I would do Old Time Dancing at the Gannon Rooms."

In the early 1980s, the houses in which Joyce Vale was living were condemned and demolished. She, her husband, and son, Kevin, relocated to Saxon Road, where she lives today. Her husband is now a resident at Aldringham Court.

In 2008, Joyce Vale became an Adherant Member of the Salvation Army. She attends services and collects on behalf of the charity although she does not wear its uniform.

"People are very kind. I get lifts to see my husband and into town when I need to go shopping. The High Street has changed, though, I think it would be nice to have somewhere like Ashfords again."

Ann Watling b.1933

Ann Watling was six when war broke out.

"I was at home and I heard it on the radio on a Sunday morning. We had to go into school to be fitted with gas masks. We carried them around with us all the time, along with our identity card. Mum made me a little bag for my gas mask with a shoulder strap. I don't think we minded carrying them about – it was what we were used to."

When Ann Watling left primary school in Saxmundham, she was 15. She went to work in the Chocolate Box, a sweet shop on the High Street, where the Pet Shop is now.

"When I was 17, I started at Leiston Works, in the Pye radio section, assembling radios for the Army and for domestic use. I worked there for about five years before I came back to Saxmundham to work in the glass factory."

The Gallenkamp factory was on Station Approach in Saxmundham and made glass instruments for use in laboratories. Eventually the factory closed and the building was demolished.

"I went to Leiston and worked in the International Stores for about 16 years. It was a long day, I'd leave home before eight and not get home until after six. My Mum was getting elderly so I came back to Sax and took a job at Tenza so that I could be closer to home."

Ann Watling had wanted to play the piano since she was a young girl.

"I went to Sunday school when I was five and loved the singing. My Mum and Dad couldn't afford to get a piano at home but my aunt in Aldeburgh did have one. I finally bought one for myself when I was at Leiston Works. I went to a lady in

Leiston for my first lessons, one hour after work once a week. When that teacher died, I used to bike to Rendham for lessons. I've been playing ever since."

Ann Watling now plays the organ at the United Reformed Church in Rendham Road every Sunday.

Acknowledgements

My sincere gratitude to everyone who helped me write this book.

Most especially to my Mum, for introducing me to so many fascinating people. To Penny and Chris, for their encouragement and continued belief in the project, and to Gabby Crick for invaluable proof-reading, kindness and support.

Also; Deborah Eidson, Bob Foyers, Sarah Pastor, Simon Milldown, Peter Minta, Angela Prichard, Saxmundham Museum, Stephen Stebbings, Dorothy Thompson, Sarah Wardle.

Belinda Moore - writer
Belinda Moore is a freelance writer. She lives in Saxmundham with her husband, Marcus Bacon, and their two sons. She is a founder and governor of Saxmundham Free School.

Penny Robertson - editor
Penny Robertson is secretary of Leiston & District Beekeepers' Association and formerly editor of the Saxmundham Town Telegraph. She lives in Saxmundham with her partner Linda Serpell.

Christopher Newson - photographer
Christopher Newson is an artist who lives in Saxmundham. His story is in this book.

Printed in Great Britain
by Amazon.co.uk, Ltd.,
Marston Gate.